EDITOR: Maryanne Blacker

FOOD EDITOR: Pamela Clark

■ ■ ■

ART DIRECTOR: Paula Wooller

DESIGNER: Robbylee Phelan

■ ■ ■

DEPUTY FOOD EDITOR: Jan Castorina

ASSISTANT FOOD EDITOR: Kathy Snowball

ASSOCIATE FOOD EDITOR: Enid Morrison

SENIOR HOME ECONOMISTS: Alexandra McCowan,
Louise Patniotis, Kathy Wharton

HOME ECONOMISTS: Cynthia Black, Leisel Chen,
Bronwen Clark, Kathy McGarry, Tracey Port,
Sophia Young

EDITORIAL COORDINATOR: Elizabeth Hooper

KITCHEN ASSISTANT: Amy Wong

■ ■ ■

STYLISTS: Lucy Andrews, Wendy Berecry,
Marie-Helene Clauzon, Carolyn Fienberg, Jane Hann,
Rosemary de Santis

PHOTOGRAPHERS: Kevin Brown, Robert Clark,
Robert Taylor, Jon Waddy

■ ■ ■

HOME LIBRARY EDITORIAL COORDINATOR:
Fiona Nicholas

■ ■ ■

ACP PUBLISHER: Richard Walsh

ACP DEPUTY PUBLISHER: Nick Chan

■ ■ ■

Produced by The Australian Women's Weekly Home Library.
Typeset by ACP Colour Graphics Pty Ltd. Colour separations
by Network Graphics Pty. Ltd. in Sydney. Printing by
Diamond Press Holdings Pty. Ltd. in Sydney.
Published by ACP Publishing Pty Ltd, 54 Park Street, Sydney.
♦ AUSTRALIA: Distributed by Network Distribution Company,
54 Park Street, Sydney, (02) 282 8777.
♦ UNITED KINGDOM: Distributed in the U.K. by Australian
Consolidated Press (UK) Ltd, 20 Galowhill Rd, Brackmills,
Northampton NN4 OEE (0604) 760 456.
♦ CANADA: Distributed in Canada by Whitecap
Books Ltd, 1086 West 3rd St,
North Vancouver V7P 3J6 (604) 980 9852.
♦ NEW ZEALAND: Distributed in New Zealand by Netlink
Distribution Company, 17B Hargreaves St, Level 5,
College Hill, Auckland 1 (9) 302 7616.
♦ SOUTH AFRICA: Distributed in South Africa by Intermag,
PO Box 57394, Springfield 2137 (011) 493 3200.

■ ■ ■

Cooking for Crowds

Includes index.
ISBN 1 86396 021 X

1. Cookery. 2. Entertaining. (Series:
Australian Women's Weekly Home
Library).

■ ■ ■

© A C P Publishing Pty Ltd 1993
ACN 053 273 546
This publication is copyright. No part of it may be reproduced
or transmitted in any form without the written permission
of the publishers.

■ ■ ■

COVER: Clockwise from back, left: Seafood Paella, page 43;
Herbed Polenta Slice, page 86; Warm Braised Leek and
Tomato Salad, page 86; Roast Veal with Mustard Fruits,
page 75; Eggplant and Goats' Cheese Roulade, page 16.
"Orofino" china and glasses from Villeroy & Boch; pewter
platter from Home & Garden on the Mall.
OPPOSITE: Prosciutto Crepe Cake, page 9.
BACK COVER: From top: Raspberry and Vanilla
Sorbet Terrine, Chocolate Mousse Cake with
Coffee Anglaise, page 104.

COOKING
— FOR —
CROWDS

"Keep it simple" is the key to s̶̶̶̶ ̶̶̶̶̶re c̶̶̶king for a crowd. Lots of our fabulous re̶̶̶̶ ̶̶̶̶̶̶l in themselves and can be made ahead — great w̶̶̶ you're short of time. For tempting menu ideas, turn to page 120, and page 122 for party planning tips. Recipes serve 10 unless otherwise specified. We suggest you make only one quantity at a time, that is, if you wish to serve two batches of the same recipe, make each batch separately as most households do not have pots and pans large enough for big quantities.

Pamela Clark

FOOD EDITOR

BRITISH & NORTH AMERICAN READERS: Please note that Australian cup and spoon measurements are metric. A quick conversion guide appears on page 127.
A glossary explaining unfamiliar terms and ingredients appears on page 123.

FINGER FOOD & STARTERS

Whether you would like next-to-no cooking or recipes that are slightly more elaborate, you will find here a superb variety of tantalising finger food, soups and starters to add pleasure to every occasion. Most can be prepared or made ahead, so you have minimum fuss at the last minute. Most recipes serve 10 people, but they can be increased as desired for larger parties.

GRAVLAX AND CARPACCIO CANAPES

1 large French bread stick, thinly sliced
60g butter, melted
1 tablespoon light olive oil
1 large red pepper
15 slices (450g) gravlax, halved
⅔ cup (160ml) black olive paste
⅓ cup (45g) drained chopped sun-dried tomatoes
1 cup (80g) parmesan cheese flakes

EGGPLANT PUREE
1 large eggplant
1 tablespoon chopped fresh thyme
2 cloves garlic, crushed
3 teaspoons lemon juice
3 teaspoons olive oil

CARPACCIO
400g piece of beef eye-fillet

Brush 1 side of each bread slice with combined butter and oil. Place bread in single layer on oven trays, toast in moderately hot oven about 10 minutes or until lightly browned and crisp.

Quarter pepper, remove seeds and membranes. Grill pepper, skin side up, until skin blisters and blackens. Peel away skin, slice pepper thinly.

Spread toast with some of the eggplant puree. Top half the toast with gravlax and some of the red pepper strips. Top remaining toast with carpaccio, some of the olive paste, tomatoes and cheese.

Eggplant Puree: Prick eggplant all over with fork, place on oven tray, bake, uncovered, in moderate oven about 1 hour or until soft; cool.

Peel and chop eggplant roughly. Process eggplant with remaining ingredients until smooth.

Carpaccio: Trim beef of all fat and sinew. Cut 6 thin slices of beef, place on large sheet of plastic. Cover with another sheet of plastic, roll gently with rolling pin until very thin. Repeat with remaining beef.

Makes about 60.

- Toast and eggplant puree can be prepared 3 days ahead, carpaccio a day ahead.
- Storage: Toast, airtight container. Eggplant puree and carpaccio, covered, separately, in refrigerator.
- Freeze: Toast suitable.
- Microwave: Not suitable.

RIGHT: From back: Carpaccio Canapes, Gravlax Canapes.

Glasses, china and crystal cake stand from Waterford Wedgwood; gold basket, tablecloth, serviettes, serviette rings and gold boxes from Morris Home & Garden Wares

ANTIPASTO PLATTERS

300g kalamata olives
100g lamb prosciutto
100g spicy salami

PICKLED OCTOPUS
2kg baby octopus
1 cup (250ml) water
1 clove garlic, crushed
1 medium onion, finely chopped
1 cup (250ml) white wine vinegar
½ cup (125ml) olive oil

PESTO SALAD
1½ cups firmly packed fresh
    basil leaves
1 tablespoon pine nuts, toasted
1 clove garlic, crushed
2 tablespoons grated
    parmesan cheese
2 tablespoons olive oil
500g bocconcini, chopped
250g cherry tomatoes, halved

ROASTED PEPPERS
4 medium yellow peppers
4 medium red peppers
½ cup (125ml) olive oil
3 cloves garlic, sliced
2 tablespoons chopped fresh parsley

Just before serving, place olives, prosciutto, salami, pickled octopus, pesto salad and roasted peppers on large platters.
Pickled Octopus: Remove and discard heads and beaks from octopus; cut octopus into quarters. Combine octopus and water in pan, simmer, covered, about 1 hour or until octopus are tender; drain, cool. Combine octopus with remaining ingredients in bowl; cover, refrigerate.
Pesto Salad: Blend or process basil, nuts, garlic, cheese and oil until well combined. Combine pesto with bocconcini and tomatoes.
Roasted Peppers: Quarter peppers, remove seeds and membranes. Grill peppers, skin side up, until skin blisters and blackens. Peel away skin, cut peppers into thin strips. Combine peppers with remaining ingredients in bowl; mix well.

Serves 10.

■ Octopus, pesto salad, and peppers can be prepared 3 days ahead.
■ Storage: Covered, separately, in refrigerator.
■ Freeze: Not suitable.
■ Microwave: Not suitable.

LEFT: Antipasto Platters.
ABOVE: Bruschetta with Easy-Mix Toppings.
Left: China from Lifestyle Imports.

BRUSCHETTA WITH EASY-MIX TOPPINGS

2 large French bread sticks
1 cup (250ml) olive oil
4 cloves garlic, crushed

BASIL TOMATO TOPPING
2 small ripe tomatoes, finely chopped
2 cloves garlic, crushed
2 tablespoons olive oil
¼ cup shredded fresh basil

OLIVE TOPPING
190g jar black olive paste
1½ tablespoons chopped
    fresh parsley
½ teaspoon grated lemon rind
1 clove garlic, crushed
1 baby onion, finely chopped

ONION ANCHOVY TOPPING
2 tablespoons olive oil
2 medium red Spanish onions,
    finely chopped
1 clove garlic, crushed
56g can anchovy fillets,
    finely chopped
2 teaspoons balsamic vinegar

Cut bread into 1cm slices, brush both sides of slices with combined oil and garlic. Place bread in single layer on oven trays, toast in moderately hot oven about 5 minutes each side or until bread is browned and crisp; cool. Serve bread with easy-mix toppings.
Basil Tomato Topping: Combine all ingredients in bowl; mix well.
Olive Topping: Combine all ingredients in bowl; mix well.
Onion Anchovy Topping: Combine all ingredients in bowl; mix well.

Serves 10.

■ Recipe can be prepared a day ahead.
■ Storage: Bruschetta, airtight container. Toppings, covered, in refrigerator.
■ Freeze: Not suitable.
■ Microwave: Not suitable.

CURRIED SESAME CHICKEN

10 chicken thigh fillets
1½ cups (375ml) plain yogurt
2 tablespoons mango chutney
2 tablespoons dry sherry
1 tablespoon sherry vinegar
1 tablespoon curry paste
1 clove garlic, crushed
1 teaspoon turmeric
¼ teaspoon ground cardamom
¼ teaspoon ground cumin
¾ cup (110g) sesame seeds, toasted

Cut chicken into 2cm pieces. Blend or process yogurt, chutney, sherry, vinegar, paste, garlic and spices until combined. Combine chicken with ¾ cup (180ml) of the marinade in bowl, cover, refrigerate 3 hours or overnight. Reserve remaining marinade for serving.

Heat large pan, add undrained chicken mixture, simmer, uncovered, stirring occasionally, about 7 minutes or until chicken is tender. Toss chicken in seeds. Serve hot or cold with reserved marinade.

Makes about 30.

- Recipe can be made a day ahead.
- Storage: Covered, in refrigerator.
- Freeze: Not suitable.
- Microwave: Not suitable.

PORK AND PRAWN ROLLS WITH DIPPING SAUCE

4 Chinese dried mushrooms
15 x 22cm square sheets of rice paper
1½ cups shredded lettuce
250g cooked shelled prawns, finely chopped
125g Chinese barbecued pork, finely chopped
¾ cup (180ml) hoi sin sauce
½ cup firmly packed fresh mint leaves

DIPPING SAUCE
⅓ cup (80ml) lime juice
2 tablespoons mild sweet chilli sauce
⅓ cup (80ml) light soy sauce
1 tablespoon sugar
2 teaspoons sesame oil

Place mushrooms in heatproof bowl, cover with boiling water, stand 20 minutes. Drain mushrooms, discard stems, slice caps finely.

Soak 1 sheet of rice paper in bowl of cold water few minutes or until limp. Place rice paper on clean tea-towel, cut rice paper in half. Top each half with a little of the lettuce, prawns, pork, sauce and mushrooms, top with a mint leaf. Roll paper up firmly, tucking in edges. Repeat with remaining ingredients. Serve rolls with dipping sauce.

Dipping Sauce: Combine all ingredients in jar; shake well.

Makes 30.

- Rolls can be made a day ahead. Dipping sauce can be made 3 days ahead.
- Storage: Covered, separately, in refrigerator.
- Freeze: Not suitable.
- Microwave: Not suitable.

ABOVE: From left: Baby Onion Tartlets, Pork and Prawn Rolls with Dipping Sauce, Curried Sesame Chicken.
RIGHT: Butter Bean and Csabai Soup.

Above: Platter from Accoutrement. Right: China from Lifestyle Imports.

BABY ONION TARTLETS

2 cups (300g) plain flour
½ teaspoon cracked black pepper
125g butter
2 eggs, lightly beaten
¼ cup (60ml) olive oil
6 medium onions, sliced
2 cloves garlic, crushed
1 tablespoon Worcestershire sauce
1 tablespoon tomato sauce
2 teaspoons sugar
2 teaspoons chopped fresh thyme
¼ cup (60ml) milk
¼ cup (60ml) cream
2 eggs, lightly beaten, extra

Grease 3 x 12-hole tart trays. Sift flour into bowl, add pepper, rub in butter, then stir in eggs. Press dough into a ball, knead gently on lightly floured surface until smooth, cover, refrigerate dough 30 minutes.

Heat oil in pan, add onions and garlic, cook, stirring, over low heat about 30 minutes or until onions are very soft. Stir in sauces, sugar and thyme; cool.

Roll pastry on lightly floured surface until 2mm thick. Cut 36 x 7.5cm rounds from pastry, place rounds in prepared trays. Divide onion mixture between pastry cases, pour over combined milk, cream and extra eggs. Bake tartlets in moderately hot oven about 15 minutes or until browned and set.

Makes 36.

- Tartlets can be made 2 days ahead.
- Storage: Covered, in refrigerator.
- Freeze: Suitable.
- Microwave: Not suitable.

BUTTER BEAN AND CSABAI SOUP

30g butter
1 medium onion, sliced
2 cloves garlic, crushed
3 litres (12 cups) chicken stock
2 tablespoons chopped fresh thyme
2 bay leaves
4 medium carrots, sliced
2 small (about 400g) csabai sausages, chopped
2 large zucchini, chopped
3 x 310g cans butter beans, rinsed, drained
1 tablespoon chopped fresh thyme, extra

Heat butter in large pan, add onion and garlic, cook, stirring, until onion is soft. Add stock, bring to boil, add thyme, bay leaves and carrots, simmer, covered, until carrots are just tender.

Add sausages to dry pan, cook, stirring, until browned and cooked through; drain on absorbent paper. Add sausages, zucchini and beans to soup, simmer, uncovered, until zucchini are tender. Discard bay leaves; stir in extra thyme.

Serves 10.

- Recipe can be made a day ahead.
- Storage: Covered, in refrigerator.
- Freeze: Not suitable.
- Microwave: Not suitable.

CHEESY FILLO PARCELS

1 cup (200g) ricotta cheese
¼ cup (20g) grated parmesan cheese
70g sliced ham, finely chopped
1 tablespoon chopped fresh chives
1 tablespoon chopped fresh basil
¼ cup (40g) chopped pitted
    black olives
1 teaspoon seeded mustard
¼ teaspoon seasoned pepper
2 egg yolks
10 sheets fillo pastry
125g butter, melted

Combine cheeses, ham, herbs, olives, mustard, pepper and egg yolks in bowl; mix well. Layer 2 sheets of pastry together, brushing each with butter, cut crossways into 7cm strips.

Place 2 level teaspoons of mixture at 1 end of each strip. Fold end over to form a triangle, continue folding to end, maintaining triangle shape; brush with a little more butter. Place triangles onto lightly greased oven trays. Repeat with remaining pastry, butter and filling.

Just before serving, bake triangles in moderate oven about 15 minutes or until lightly browned.

Makes about 35.

■ Triangles can be prepared
    a day ahead.
■ Storage: Covered, in refrigerator.
■ Freeze: Uncooked triangles suitable.
■ Microwave: Not suitable.

WITLOF WITH SMOKED CHICKEN AND AVOCADO

3 medium witlof

FILLING
½ cup (125ml) sour cream
1½ tablespoons bottled
    Italian dressing
1 cup (about 150g) chopped
    smoked chicken
1½ tablespoons chopped
    fresh chives
1 large avocado, chopped

Separate witlof leaves, trim ends. Divide filling between leaves, cover, refrigerate until ready to serve.

Filling: Combine cream, dressing, chicken and chives in bowl, stir in avocado.

Makes about 30.

■ Filling, without avocado, can be
    made a day ahead.
■ Storage: Covered, in refrigerator.
■ Freeze: Not suitable.

MINI LAMB KEBABS

500g lamb fillets
¼ cup (60ml) olive oil
¼ cup (60ml) lemon juice
2 cloves garlic, crushed
1 tablespoon chopped
    fresh rosemary
1 tablespoon chopped fresh oregano
1 teaspoon seasoned pepper
2 teaspoons Dijon mustard
¼ cup (60ml) olive oil, extra

Cut lamb into thin strips. Pound strips lightly to flatten, cut into 4cm lengths. Thread strips onto 30 small skewers, about 13cm long. Place kebabs in shallow dish, pour over combined oil, juice, garlic, herbs, pepper and mustard. Cover, refrigerate several hours or overnight.

Drain lamb from marinade, reserve marinade. Heat extra oil in large pan, add kebabs in batches, cook over high heat until lamb is browned and just tender; remove kebabs from pan. Add reserved marinade to pan, bring to boil. Pour over kebabs, serve warm or cold.

Makes 30.

■ Recipe can be prepared a day ahead.
■ Storage: Covered, in refrigerator.
■ Freeze: Uncooked, marinated
    lamb suitable.
■ Microwave: Not suitable.

PROSCIUTTO CREPE CAKE

1¼ cups (185g) plain flour
5 eggs
1 tablespoon light olive oil
2 cups (500ml) milk
30 slices (about 300g) prosciutto

CHEESE SAUCE
200g butter
1 clove garlic, crushed
1 cup (150g) plain flour
1 litre (4 cups) milk
1 tablespoon chopped fresh thyme
1 tablespoon chopped fresh sage
1 cup (80g) grated parmesan cheese
1 teaspoon seasoned pepper

Process flour, eggs, oil and milk until smooth, cover, stand 1 hour. Pour 2 tablespoons of mixture into heated greased heavy-based crepe pan, cook until lightly browned underneath. Turn crepe, brown other side. Repeat with remaining batter. You will need 18 crepes for this recipe.

Spread 1 crepe with some of the cheese sauce, sprinkle with 2 slices of chopped prosciutto. Repeat layering with 4 more crepes, cheese sauce and prosciutto, finishing with a crepe. Make 2 more cakes with remaining crepes, sauce and prosciutto. Cover, refrigerate about 1 hour or until firm. Cut into wedges to serve.

Cheese Sauce: Heat butter and garlic in pan, add flour, stir over heat until bubbling. Remove pan from heat, gradually stir in milk. Stir over heat until mixture boils and thickens, add herbs, cheese and pepper, stir over heat until cheese is melted. Cover surface of sauce with plastic wrap; cool until thick.

Makes 3.

- Recipe can be made 2 days ahead.
- Storage: Covered, in refrigerator.
- Freeze: Crepes suitable.
- Microwave: Cheese sauce suitable.

LEFT: Clockwise from left: Witlof with Smoked Chicken and Avocado, Cheesy Fillo Parcels, Mini Lamb Kebabs.
RIGHT: Prosciutto Crepe Cake.

Left: China from Villeroy & Boch; glasses and basket from Home & Garden on the Mall.

CHEESE AND SALAMI ROLLS

2 sheets ready-rolled puff pastry
1 egg, lightly beaten
1 teaspoon poppy seeds

FILLING
1 tablespoon vegetable oil
1 medium onion, chopped
100g mild salami, chopped
2 medium zucchini, grated
1 medium carrot, grated
½ cup (40g) grated parmesan cheese
1 tablespoon chopped fresh oregano
2 tablespoons chopped pitted
    black olives
⅓ cup (65g) ricotta cheese

Cut each sheet of pastry into 3 strips. Divide filling evenly along centre of each strip, brush edges with some of the egg. Roll pastry over to enclose filling. Trim ends, cut each strip into 5 pieces. Place rolls onto greased oven tray, seam side down. Brush with remaining egg, sprinkle with seeds. Bake in hot oven about 10 minutes or until lightly browned and crisp.
Filling: Heat oil in pan, add onion, salami, zucchini and carrot, cook, stirring, until onion is soft, cool to room temperature. Combine onion mixture with remaining ingredients in bowl; mix well.

Makes 30.

- ■ Rolls can be made a day ahead.
- ■ Storage: Covered, in refrigerator.
- ■ Freeze: Uncooked rolls suitable.
- ■ Microwave: Not suitable.

PROSCIUTTO AND CHEESE BITES

30 small basil leaves
15 baby bocconcini cheese, halved
30 slices (about 300g) prosciutto
30 cherry tomatoes

DRESSING
¼ cup (60ml) olive oil
1 tablespoon balsamic vinegar
¼ teaspoon sugar

Place a basil leaf and a piece of cheese at 1 end of each prosciutto slice. Roll up, folding in sides to enclose filling. Place on toothpicks with tomatoes.

Just before serving, place on oven trays, bake in very hot oven about 3 minutes or until cheese is just soft. Drizzle with dressing before serving.
Dressing: Combine all ingredients in jar; shake well.

Makes 30.

- ■ Recipe can be prepared a day ahead. Dressing can be made a day ahead.
- ■ Storage: Covered, separately, in refrigerator.
- ■ Freeze: Not suitable.
- ■ Microwave: Not suitable.

PEPPERONI FRITATTA SLICE

50g butter
⅓ cup (80ml) olive oil
1kg new potatoes, thinly sliced
1 tablespoon olive oil, extra
2 medium red Spanish
    onions, chopped
2 cloves garlic, crushed
100g pepperoni, chopped
2 tablespoons chopped
    fresh rosemary
10 eggs, lightly beaten
½ cup (125ml) milk

Lightly grease 20cm x 30cm lamington pan. Heat half the butter and half the oil in pan, add potatoes in batches, cook until well browned on both sides (add remaining butter and oil when necessary); drain on absorbent paper. Heat extra oil in pan, add onions and garlic, cook, stirring, until onions are very soft.

Layer half the potatoes in prepared pan, sprinkle with onion mixture, pepperoni and half the rosemary, top with remaining potatoes. Pour combined eggs and milk over potatoes, sprinkle with remaining rosemary. Bake, uncovered, in moderate oven about 35 minutes or until firm and browned; cool. Cover, refrigerate several hours before cutting.

Serves 10.

- ■ Recipe can be made 2 days ahead.
- ■ Storage: Covered, in refrigerator.
- ■ Freeze: Not suitable.
- ■ Microwave: Not suitable.

LEFT: Clockwise from left: Cheese and Salami Rolls, Pepperoni Frittata Slice, Prosciutto and Cheese Bites.
China and tin dish from Home & Garden on the Mall.

SEAFOOD SALAD WITH ROASTED GARLIC DRESSING

3 medium red peppers
1kg small mussels
½ cup (125ml) dry white wine
1.5kg medium uncooked prawns
500g scallops
400g calamari tubes, chopped
1 large red Spanish onion, sliced
½ cup (80g) chopped pitted
**   green olives**
½ cup (80g) chopped pitted
**   black olives**
1 cup firmly packed flat-leafed
**   parsley leaves**
½ cup shredded fresh basil
3 bunches (about 360g) rocket

ROASTED GARLIC DRESSING
1 bulb (about 80g) garlic
½ cup (125ml) lemon juice
½ cup (125ml) virgin olive oil
1 teaspoon sugar

Quarter peppers, remove seeds and membranes. Grill peppers, skin side up, until skin blisters and blackens. Peel away skin, slice peppers. Scrub mussels, remove beards. Heat wine in large pan, add mussels, cook, covered, few minutes or until shells open; drain. Remove mussels from shells, discard shells.

Shell and devein prawns, leaving tails intact. Cook prawns, scallops, calamari and onion on barbecue or heated greased pan in batches until just tender. Combine peppers, seafood, onion, olives, parsley and basil in bowl, add dressing; mix well. Serve with rocket.

Roasted Garlic Dressing: Place unpeeled garlic bulb on oven tray, bake, uncovered, in moderate oven about 1 hour or until soft; cool. Cut bulb in half, squeeze garlic from skins, push through sieve. Combine garlic puree, juice, oil and sugar in jar; shake well.

Serves 10.

■ Recipe can be made a day ahead.
■ Storage: Covered, in refrigerator.
■ Freeze: Not suitable.
■ Microwave: Not suitable.

SPINACH AND PASTA TERRINE

20 slices (about 200g) prosciutto
1 tablespoon olive oil
2 cloves garlic, crushed
⅓ cup (45g) drained sliced
**   sun-dried tomatoes**
1 bunch (about 650g) English spinach
4 eggs, lightly beaten
1 cup (250ml) cream
250g coloured spiral pasta
1 cup (125g) grated tasty
**   cheddar cheese**
½ cup (40g) grated parmesan cheese
½ cup chopped fresh basil

TOMATO PUREE
3 large tomatoes, peeled, seeded
3 teaspoons white vinegar
1 teaspoon sugar

Grease 14cm x 21cm loaf pan, cover base with paper, grease paper. Line base and sides of pan with 14 slices of prosciutto. Heat oil in pan, add garlic, tomatoes and spinach, cook until spinach is wilted, cool 5 minutes. Process spinach mixture, eggs and cream until smooth.

Add pasta to pan of boiling water, boil, uncovered, until tender; drain, rinse under cold water, drain well.

Combine spinach mixture, pasta, cheeses and basil in bowl; mix well. Spoon mixture into prepared pan, top with remaining prosciutto, cover with foil. Place pan in baking dish with enough boiling water to come halfway up sides of pan. Bake in moderate oven 1¼ hours. Remove pan from water, return pan to oven, bake about further 30 minutes or until cooked; cool. Cover, refrigerate until firm. Serve sliced with tomato puree.

Tomato Puree: Blend or process all ingredients until smooth; strain.

Serves 10.

■ Terrine best made a day ahead, can be made 2 days ahead. Tomato puree can be made a day ahead.
■ Storage: Covered, separately, in refrigerator.
■ Freeze: Not suitable.
■ Microwave: Pasta suitable.

LEFT: From back: Seafood Salad with Roasted Garlic Dressing, Spinach and Pasta Terrine.
BELOW: Spicy Marinated Octopus.
Below: Platter from Accoutrement.

SPICY MARINATED OCTOPUS

2kg baby octopus
1 tablespoon light olive oil
2 cloves garlic, crushed
½ cup (125ml) mild sweet chilli sauce
2 tablespoons light soy sauce
1 teaspoon grated fresh ginger
2 tablespoons chopped fresh thyme
¼ cup (60ml) light olive oil, extra
1 tablespoon red wine vinegar
1 bunch (about 650g) English spinach
1 red oak leaf lettuce
150g snow pea sprouts

Remove and discard heads and beaks from octopus; cut octopus into quarters. Heat oil in pan, add octopus in batches, cook quickly over high heat until well browned and tender. Place hot octopus in bowl, stir in combined garlic, sauces, ginger, thyme, extra oil and vinegar; cool. Cover, refrigerate overnight.

Drain octopus, reserve marinade. Serve octopus on spinach leaves, torn lettuce leaves and snow pea sprouts; drizzle with reserved marinade.

Serves 10.

■ Octopus can be marinated a day ahead.
■ Storage: Covered, in refrigerator.
■ Freeze: Not suitable.
■ Microwave: Not suitable.

CHICKEN AND AVOCADO CREPE PARCELS

5 bacon rashers, chopped
1 tablespoon vegetable oil
1 medium onion, sliced
60g butter
⅓ cup (50g) plain flour
1¾ cups (430ml) milk
1½ tablespoons seeded mustard
1 cup (125g) grated tasty
cheddar cheese
3 cups (450g) chopped
cooked chicken
4 green shallots, chopped
2 medium avocados, sliced

CREPES
5 eggs
1 cup (150g) plain flour
2 cups (500ml) milk
2 tablespoons vegetable oil

HERB CREAM
300ml sour cream
2 tablespoons milk
4 green shallots, finely chopped
2 tablespoons shredded fresh basil

Add bacon to pan, cook, stirring, until crisp; drain on absorbent paper. Heat oil in pan, add onion, cook, stirring, until soft; drain on absorbent paper.

Heat butter in pan, add flour, cook, stirring, until dry and grainy. Remove from heat, stir in milk, stir over heat until mixture boils and thickens. Remove from heat, stir in mustard and cheese, then bacon, onion, chicken and shallots.

Place 2 tablespoons of chicken mixture at 1 end of each crepe, top with a slice of avocado, roll up, tucking in ends to form parcels. Place parcels, seam side down, onto lightly greased oven trays, bake in moderately hot oven about 15 minutes or until browned and heated through. Serve with herb cream.

Crepes: Combine all ingredients in bowl, whisk until smooth (or, blend or process until smooth); stand 5 minutes. Pour 2 to 3 tablespoons of batter into heated greased heavy-based crepe pan. Cook until browned underneath, turn crepe, brown other side. Repeat with remaining batter. You will need 20 crepes for this recipe.

Herb Cream: Combine all ingredients in bowl; mix well.

Serves 10.

- Recipe can be prepared a day ahead.
- Storage: Uncooked, filled crepes and herb cream, covered, separately, in refrigerator.
- Freeze: Crepes suitable.
- Microwave: Not suitable.

MUSHROOM STRUDELS WITH GARLIC MAYONNAISE

12 sheets fillo pastry
60g butter, melted
2 tablespoons stale breadcrumbs

FILLING
60g butter, melted
1.5kg flat mushrooms, sliced
2 cloves garlic, crushed
½ cup shredded fresh basil
½ cup (80g) pine nuts, toasted

GARLIC MAYONNAISE
1 egg
1 tablespoon lemon juice
1 clove garlic, crushed
1 cup (250ml) light olive oil

Layer 6 sheets of pastry together, brushing each sheet with butter. Mould half the filling along centre of pastry in a 10cm x 30cm rectangle. Fold over and roll up pastry to enclose filling. Place strudel, seam side down, on greased oven tray. Repeat with remaining pastry, butter and filling. Brush strudels with remaining butter, sprinkle with breadcrumbs.

Just before serving, bake in moderately hot oven about 20 minutes or until browned. Serve with garlic mayonnaise.

Filling: Heat butter in large pan, add mushrooms and garlic, cook, stirring, until mushrooms are very soft and liquid evaporated. Stir in basil and nuts; cool.

Garlic Mayonnaise: Process egg, juice and garlic until smooth. Gradually add oil in a thin stream while motor is operating; process until thick.

Serves 10.

- Strudels can be prepared a day ahead. Mayonnaise can be made 2 days ahead.
- Storage: Covered, separately, in refrigerator.
- Freeze: Not suitable.
- Microwave: Not suitable.

PESTO CHEESECAKE WITH CARAWAY CRACKERS

2 tablespoons stale breadcrumbs
375g packaged cream cheese
¾ cup (150g) ricotta cheese
½ teaspoon seasoned pepper
3 eggs
½ cup (125ml) bottled pesto
¼ cup (25g) drained chopped
    sun-dried tomatoes
1 tablespoon chopped fresh chives
¼ cup (40g) pine nuts

CARAWAY CRACKERS
1 tablespoon vegetable oil
1 medium onion, grated
1½ cups (225g) plain flour
1 teaspoon dry mustard
125g butter, chopped
3 teaspoons caraway seeds
½ cup (40g) grated parmesan cheese
1 egg yolk
1 egg, lightly beaten
½ teaspoon garlic powder
1 teaspoon fine sea salt

Cover base of 20cm springform tin with foil, grease base and side, sprinkle with breadcrumbs. Beat cheeses in small bowl with electric mixer until light, add pepper and eggs 1 at a time; beat until combined. Divide mixture in half. Add pesto to 1 half of mixture, and tomatoes and chives to remaining half; mix well.

Spread pesto mixture over base of prepared tin, top evenly with tomato mixture, sprinkle with nuts. Place tin on oven tray, bake in moderately slow oven about 50 minutes or until set; cool. Cover, refrigerate until firm. Serve at room temperature with caraway crackers.

Caraway Crackers: Heat oil in pan, add onion, cook, stirring, until soft and lightly browned. Sift flour and mustard into bowl, rub in butter. Stir in onion, seeds, cheese and egg yolk, mix to a firm dough. Knead on lightly floured surface until smooth. Cover, refrigerate 30 minutes.

Roll dough between 2 sheets of baking paper until 3mm thick. Cut 4cm squares from pastry. Place squares on greased oven trays, brush with egg, sprinkle with garlic powder and salt. Bake crackers in moderately hot oven about 12 minutes or until lightly browned; cool on trays.

Serves about 20.

■ Recipe can be made 2 days ahead.
■ Storage: Cheesecake, covered, in refrigerator. Caraway crackers, airtight container.
■ Freeze: Not suitable.
■ Microwave: Not suitable.

POLENTA WITH CREAMY HERB TOPPING

2⅔ cups (660ml) chicken stock
1 cup (150g) polenta
1 cup (80g) grated parmesan cheese
1 egg, lightly beaten
plain flour
vegetable oil for deep-frying
¼ cup (25g) drained sliced
    sun-dried tomatoes
1 tablespoon finely shredded
    fresh basil

CREAMY HERB TOPPING
½ cup (125ml) sour cream
1 tablespoon chopped fresh basil
1 tablespoon chopped fresh chives
1 small clove garlic, crushed

Grease 20cm x 30cm lamington pan. Bring stock to boil in pan, gradually add polenta, simmer, stirring, about 10 minutes or until soft and thick. Remove from heat, stir in cheese and egg. Press firmly into prepared pan, cover, refrigerate several hours or until firm.

Turn polenta out of pan, cut into 30 diamond shapes, toss in flour, shake away excess flour. Deep-fry polenta in batches in hot oil until lightly browned, drain on absorbent paper; cool. Top polenta with creamy herb topping, tomatoes and basil.

Creamy Herb Topping: Combine all ingredients in bowl; mix well.

Makes 30.

■ Polenta and topping can be prepared a day ahead.
■ Storage: Covered, in refrigerator.
■ Freeze: Polenta suitable.
■ Microwave: Not suitable.

LEFT: From back: Mushroom Strudels with Garlic Mayonnaise, Chicken and Avocado Crepe Parcels.
BELOW: From back: Pesto Cheesecake with Caraway Crackers, Polenta with Creamy Herb Topping.

Left: Plates from Accoutrement. Below: China from Lifestyle Imports; tin plate and glasses from Home & Garden on the Mall.

VEAL AND BACON TERRINE

10 thin bacon rashers
2 medium white onions,
   finely chopped
1½ cups chopped fresh parsley
550g (about 6) veal schnitzels
12 thin bacon rashers, extra
3 bay leaves
⅔ cup (160ml) dry white wine

CUMBERLAND SAUCE
1 medium lemon
1 medium orange
2 tablespoons lemon juice
¼ cup (60ml) orange juice
2 tablespoons redcurrant jelly
¼ cup (60ml) port
½ teaspoon French mustard
2 green shallots, chopped

Remove rind from all bacon rashers. Line 11cm x 21cm loaf dish (1.5 litre/6 cup capacity) with 10 slices of bacon, allowing ends to overhang edges of dish. Combine onions and parsley in bowl. Place quarter of the veal over base of dish, top with a third of the parsley mixture, press down firmly. Top with 4 of the extra bacon rashers.

Continue layering with remaining veal, parsley mixture and extra bacon, finishing with veal. Fold ends of bacon over to enclose filling, top with bay leaves. Pour wine over terrine, cover dish with foil, place in baking dish with enough boiling water to come halfway up sides of dish. Bake in moderate oven about 1½ hours or until firm; drain excess liquid from terrine; cool.

Cover terrine with plastic wrap, press weight on top of terrine, refrigerate until cold. Serve with cumberland sauce.

Cumberland Sauce: Using a vegetable peeler, peel rind thinly from lemon and orange. Cut rind into thin strips. Place rind in pan, cover with water, boil, uncovered, 3 minutes; drain. Combine rind, juices, jelly, port and mustard in pan, simmer, uncovered, 2 minutes, stir in shallots; cool.

Serves 10.

- Terrine best made a day ahead. Cumberland sauce can be made a day ahead.
- Storage: Covered, in refrigerator.
- Freeze: Not suitable.
- Microwave: Sauce suitable.

EGGPLANT AND GOATS' CHEESE ROULADE

2 large red peppers
700g goats' cheese, chopped
250g packet cream cheese, chopped
½ cup firmly packed fresh
   basil leaves
½ cup (65g) drained chopped
   sun-dried tomatoes
3 medium eggplants
vegetable oil for shallow-frying
3 cups (150g) firmly packed
   watercress sprigs
500g cherry tomatoes, halved
1 cup (180g) baby black olives
⅓ cup (50g) pine nuts, toasted
½ cup (90g) drained capers

DRESSING
½ cup (125ml) balsamic vinegar
¾ cup (180ml) virgin olive oil
1 clove garlic, crushed

Quarter peppers, remove seeds and membranes. Grill peppers, skin side up, until skin blisters and blackens. Peel away skin, slice peppers. Process combined cheeses until smooth.

Place a large sheet of foil on each of 2 oven trays, grease foil. Top each piece of foil with 2 sheets of plastic wrap. Divide cheese mixture in half. Spread both mixtures into 2 x 20cm x 28cm rectangles, refrigerate 1 hour.

Place red peppers along short side of rectangles, top with basil leaves, then sun-dried tomatoes. Roll up from short side like a Swiss roll, twist ends of foil, refrigerate 1 hour or until firm.

Cut eggplants lengthways into 7mm-thick slices. Shallow-fry eggplants in hot oil until lightly browned, drain on absorbent paper; cool.

Place 2 large sheets of foil on bench, top each with 2 sheets of plastic wrap. Place eggplant slices in overlapping rows to form 2 x 23cm x 28cm rectangles on the plastic.

Unwrap cheese rolls, place on a long side of each eggplant rectangle, roll eggplant around cheese rolls, twist ends of foil, refrigerate several hours or overnight.

Before serving, trim ends of roulade. Serve roulade sliced with watercress, cherry tomatoes, olives, pine nuts and capers; drizzle with dressing.

Dressing: Combine all ingredients in jar; shake well.

Serves 10.

- Recipe can be made 3 days ahead.
- Storage: Covered, in refrigerator.
- Freeze: Not suitable.
- Microwave: Not suitable.

RIGHT: From left: Eggplant and Goats' Cheese Roulade, Veal and Bacon Terrine.

VEGETABLE RAVIOLI WITH HAZELNUT BUTTER

3 eggs
1¾ cups (260g) plain flour
¼ cup (20g) grated parmesan cheese
¾ teaspoon cracked black pepper
1 egg, lightly beaten, extra

CORN FILLING
2 fresh corn cobs
1 large carrot
30g butter
1 medium onion, finely chopped
¼ cup shredded fresh basil
⅓ cup (80ml) sour cream
salt, pepper

HAZELNUT BUTTER
250g butter, chopped
1 cup (150g) roasted hazelnuts, roughly chopped
¼ cup chopped fresh chives

Process eggs, flour, cheese and pepper until mixture forms a ball. Knead dough gently on lightly floured surface until smooth.

Cut dough into quarters, roll each quarter through pasta machine set on thickest setting. Fold dough in half, roll through machine. Repeat folding and rolling several times until dough is very smooth and elastic, dusting dough with a little extra flour, when necessary. Roll each quarter until 2mm thick rectangle.

Place 2 tablespoons of corn filling 10cm apart over 2 sheets of pasta; flatten filling slightly. Brush remaining sheets of pasta with some of the extra egg, place over filling, press firmly between filling and along edges of pasta. Cut into square ravioli shapes; lightly sprinkle with flour. You need 5 large ravioli from each sheet.

Add ravioli to large pan of boiling water, boil, uncovered, about 5 minutes or until just tender; drain. Serve ravioli with hazelnut butter.

Corn Filling: Heat heavy-based frying pan, add corn cobs, cook until browned all over, remove from heat; cool. Cut corn kernels from cobs. Cut carrot into thin strips. Heat butter in pan, add carrot and onion, cook, covered, about 10 minutes or until vegetables are tender; cool. Combine corn, onion mixture, basil and sour cream in bowl; mix well, season to taste with salt and pepper.

Hazelnut Butter: Heat large pan, add butter and hazelnuts, stir quickly over heat until butter is melted; stir in chives.

Makes 10.

- Corn filling can be made a day ahead. Ravioli can be cooked a day ahead, store on lightly oiled oven trays. Brush ravioli lightly with oil, cover with plastic wrap. Reheat in boiling water 2 to 3 minutes just before serving.
- Storage: Covered, in refrigerator.
- Freeze: Not suitable.
- Microwave: Hazelnut butter suitable.

ORIENTAL PRAWN AND CUCUMBER SOUP

40g Chinese dried mushrooms
3 litres (12 cups) chicken stock
2 tablespoons chopped fresh ginger
2 cloves garlic, chopped
4 green shallots, sliced
2 tablespoons chopped fresh chives
½ teaspoon sesame oil
2 long thin green cucumbers
2 x 227g cans water chestnuts, drained, chopped
650g (about 40) medium cooked prawns, shelled

Place mushrooms in heatproof bowl, cover with boiling water, stand 20 minutes. Drain mushrooms, discard stems, slice caps. Combine stock, ginger, garlic, shallots, chives and oil in large pan, simmer, uncovered, 3 minutes.

Using a vegetable peeler, peel long thin strips from cucumber; discard seeds. Add mushrooms, cucumber, water chestnuts and prawns to soup, stir until heated through. Serve hot or cold.

Serves 10.

- Recipe can be made a day ahead.
- Storage: Covered, in refrigerator.
- Freeze: Not suitable.
- Microwave: Suitable.

POTATO WATERCRESS SOUP

90g butter
2 medium onions, chopped
4 cloves garlic, crushed
2.25 litres (9 cups) chicken stock
4 large potatoes, chopped
2 large bunches (about 450g) watercress
300ml cream

Heat butter in pan, add onions and garlic, cook, stirring, until onions are very soft. Add stock, bring to boil, add potatoes, simmer, covered, about 10 minutes or until potatoes are soft.

Add watercress, stir over heat until just wilted. Blend or process mixture until smooth. Return to pan, add cream, stir until heated through.

Serves 10.

- Soup can be made a day ahead.
- Storage: Covered, in refrigerator.
- Freeze: Not suitable.
- Microwave: Suitable.

RIGHT: From back: Oriental Prawn and Cucumber Soup, Potato Watercress Soup. BELOW: Vegetable Ravioli with Hazelnut Butter.

Right: Bowls from Accoutrement. Below: Plates, candlesticks and basket from Lifestyle Imports; cutlery, glasses and wine basket from The Bay Tree Kitchen Shop.

CRAB GAZPACHO

5 slices white bread
vegetable oil for shallow-frying
9 large (about 2.2kg) ripe tomatoes,
 peeled, chopped
1 medium onion, chopped
2 cloves garlic, crushed
2 small green cucumbers, peeled,
 seeded, chopped
3 teaspoons tarragon vinegar
2 tablespoons chopped
 fresh tarragon
2 tablespoons virgin olive oil
1 teaspoon sugar
few drops tabasco sauce
1 cup (250ml) chicken stock

CRAB TOPPING
2 x 170g cans crab meat, drained
2 small green cucumbers, peeled,
 seeded, chopped
1 medium red Spanish onion,
 finely chopped
2 teaspoons tarragon vinegar
2 tablespoons chopped fresh parsley
2 tablespoons virgin olive oil

Remove crusts from bread, cut bread into 1cm cubes. Shallow-fry bread in hot oil until browned; drain on absorbent paper.

Process tomatoes, onion, garlic and cucumbers in batches until smooth. Combine tomato mixture, vinegar, tarragon, oil, sugar, tabasco and stock in bowl; mix well. Cover, refrigerate until cold. Serve gazpacho sprinkled with croutons and crab topping.

Crab Topping: Combine all ingredients in bowl; mix well.

Serves 10.

- Soup and topping can be made a day ahead. Croutons can be made 4 days ahead.
- Storage: Soup and topping, covered, separately, in refrigerator. Croutons, airtight container.
- Freeze: Croutons suitable.
- Microwave: Not suitable.

PUMPKIN SOUP WITH ONION AND BACON ROLLS

1 tablespoon vegetable oil
2 medium onions, sliced
4 bacon rashers, chopped
1 clove garlic, crushed
1 tablespoon chopped fresh thyme
1.5 litres (6 cups) water
1½ cups (375ml) chicken stock
1 medium onion, chopped, extra
700g peeled pumpkin, chopped
2 medium potatoes, chopped
1 tablespoon chopped fresh chives
2 teaspoons Dijon mustard
2 teaspoons chicken stock powder
½ cup (125ml) cream

ONION AND BACON ROLLS
2 teaspoons (7g) dried yeast
½ cup (125ml) warm milk
¼ teaspoon sugar
2 cups (300g) plain flour
1 teaspoon salt
¼ cup (60ml) water
1 tablespoon unprocessed bran

Heat oil in pan, add onions, bacon and garlic, cook, stirring, until onions are soft; stir in thyme. Reserve half the bacon mixture for onion and bacon rolls.

Combine water, stock, extra onion, pumpkin and potatoes in pan, simmer, covered, about 30 minutes or until vegetables are soft. Process vegetable mixture in batches until smooth. Combine puree with remaining bacon mixture, chives, mustard, stock powder and cream, stir over heat until heated through. Serve with onion and bacon rolls.

Onion and Bacon Rolls: Combine yeast, milk and sugar in small bowl, cover, stand in warm place about 10 minutes or until mixture is frothy.

Sift flour and salt into large bowl, add reserved bacon mixture, yeast mixture and water, mix to a soft dough. Knead dough on floured surface about 5 minutes or until smooth and elastic. Place dough in oiled bowl, cover, stand in warm place about 50 minutes or until doubled in size. Divide dough into 10 portions.

Knead each portion until smooth, shape into rolls. Place rolls on lightly greased oven trays. Cover rolls, stand in warm place about 30 minutes or until doubled in size. Brush tops of rolls with a little extra milk, sprinkle with bran. Bake rolls in moderate oven about 20 minutes, or until lightly browned and sound hollow when tapped.

Serves 10.

■ Soup and rolls can be made a day ahead.
■ Storage: Soup, covered, in refrigerator. Rolls, airtight container.
■ Freeze: Rolls suitable.
■ Microwave: Soup suitable.

PAELLA-ETTES

1 tablespoon olive oil
1 cup (200g) short-grain rice
1 small onion, finely chopped
1 bay leaf
2 cloves garlic, crushed
1½ cups (375ml) chicken stock
1 teaspoon turmeric
80g salami, chopped
80g smoked ham, chopped
1 teaspoon seeded mustard
1 egg, lightly beaten
vegetable oil for deep-frying

Heat oil in pan, add rice, cook, stirring, until coated with oil. Stir in onion, bay leaf, garlic, stock and turmeric, simmer, covered, over low heat 10 minutes. Remove from heat, stand, covered, about 10 minutes or until liquid is absorbed; cool.

Blend or process salami and ham until finely minced. Combine rice, salami mixture, mustard and egg in bowl; mix well. With wet hands, mould level tablespoons of mixture into balls, cover, refrigerate 20 minutes.

Just before serving, deep-fry paella-ettes in hot oil until well browned; drain on absorbent paper.

Makes about 36.

■ Recipe can be prepared a day ahead.
■ Storage: Covered, in refrigerator.
■ Freeze: Not suitable.
■ Microwave: Not suitable.

SMOKED CHICKEN AND OLIVE TARTLETS

20 slices white bread
80g butter, melted
250g smoked chicken, chopped
300ml sour cream
¼ cup (40g) chopped pitted black olives
2 tablespoons drained chopped sun-dried tomatoes
1 tablespoon drained chopped capers
1 tablespoon chopped fresh chives
1 tablespoon chopped fresh dill
2 tablespoons chopped pitted black olives, extra
fresh dill sprigs, extra

Grease 20 holes of 2 x 12-hole deep patty pan trays. Cut an 8cm round from each slice of bread. Brush 1 side of bread rounds with butter. Press unbuttered side of bread rounds into prepared trays. Bake in moderately hot oven about 15 minutes or until lightly browned; cool.

Combine chicken, cream, olives, tomatoes, capers and herbs in bowl; mix well. Divide mixture between tartlet cases, sprinkle with extra olives, top with extra dill.

Makes 20.

■ Filling and bread cases can be made a day ahead.
■ Storage: Filling, covered, in refrigerator. Bread cases, airtight container.
■ Freeze: Not suitable.
■ Microwave: Not suitable.

LEFT: From left: Pumpkin Soup with Onion and Bacon Rolls, Crab Gazpacho.
ABOVE: From back: Paella-ettes, Smoked Chicken and Olive Tartlets.

Above: Plate and glassware from Accoutrement.

MEXICAN SALSA PLATTER

30 x 15cm flour tortillas
vegetable oil for deep-frying
1 teaspoon paprika
1 teaspoon celery salt
1 teaspoon ground cumin

CORN DIP
1 tablespoon light olive oil
1 medium red Spanish
    onion, chopped
1 clove garlic, crushed
1½ teaspoons ground cumin
125g packet cream cheese
½ cup (125ml) sour cream
130g can creamed corn
130g can corn kernels, drained
1 tablespoon mild sweet chilli sauce
1 tablespoon chopped
    fresh coriander

SALSA
2 medium tomatoes, peeled, seeded,
    finely chopped
1 medium red Spanish onion,
    finely chopped
2 tablespoons lime juice
½ teaspoon sugar
1 tablespoon chopped
    fresh coriander

GUACAMOLE
2 small avocados
2 teaspoons chopped fresh coriander
1½ tablespoons lime juice
1 tablespoon sweet chilli sauce

Cut tortillas into quarters. Deep-fry tortillas in batches in hot oil until lightly browned and crisp; drain on absorbent paper. Sprinkle with combined paprika, celery salt and cumin. Serve with corn dip, salsa and guacamole.
Corn Dip: Heat oil in pan, add onion, garlic and cumin, cook, stirring, until onion is soft; cool. Beat cream cheese and sour cream in small bowl with electric mixer until smooth, stir in onion mixture and remaining ingredients.
Salsa: Combine all ingredients in bowl; mix well.
Guacamole: Mash avocados in bowl with fork, stir in remaining ingredients. Cover surface of avocado mixture with plastic wrap until ready to serve.

Serves 10.
■ Recipe can be made a day ahead.
■ Storage: Dip, salsa and guacamole, covered, in refrigerator. Tortillas, airtight container.
■ Freeze: Not suitable.
■ Microwave: Not suitable.

MUSSELS WITH GARLIC PEPPER MAYONNAISE

40 (about 1kg) small mussels
½ cup (125ml) water
½ cup (125ml) dry white wine

GARLIC PEPPER MAYONNAISE
2 medium red peppers
2 cloves garlic, crushed
1 tablespoon mild sweet chilli sauce
1 tablespoon mayonnaise
tiny pinch ground saffron

HERB BREADCRUMBS
60g butter
1 cup (70g) stale breadcrumbs
1 clove garlic, crushed
1 tablespoon chopped fresh parsley
1 tablespoon chopped fresh chives

Scrub mussels, remove beards. Heat water and wine in large pan, add mussels, cook, covered, over high heat few minutes or until shells open. Drain, discard liquid and any unopened mussels. Remove and discard half of each mussel shell, loosen mussels in remaining shells. Top cold mussels with garlic pepper mayonnaise and herb breadcrumbs.
Garlic Pepper Mayonnaise: Quarter peppers, remove seeds and membranes. Grill peppers, skin side up, until skin blisters and blackens; peel away skin. Blend or process peppers, garlic, sauce, mayonnaise and saffron until smooth.
Herb Breadcrumbs: Heat butter in pan, add breadcrumbs, garlic and herbs, cook, stirring, until lightly browned.

Serves 10.
■ Recipe can be prepared a day ahead.
■ Storage: Mussels and mayonnaise, covered, separately in refrigerator. Breadcrumbs, airtight container.
■ Freeze: Not suitable.
■ Microwave: Mussels suitable.

FRESH OYSTERS WITH CAPER SAUCE

30 fresh oysters
½ medium red pepper
2 teaspoons finely chopped capers
2 teaspoons finely chopped gherkins
1 clove garlic, crushed
½ teaspoon coriander seeds, cracked
few drops tabasco sauce
2 tablespoons extra virgin olive oil
1 tablespoon chopped fresh parsley
½ teaspoon lemon juice

Remove oysters from shells, wash and dry shells; drain oysters on absorbent paper. Remove seeds and membranes from pepper. Grill pepper, skin side up, until skin blisters and blackens. Peel away skin, finely chop pepper.
    Combine pepper, capers, gherkins, garlic, seeds, tabasco, oil, parsley and juice in bowl; mix well. Return oysters to shells, top with pepper mixture.

Makes 30.
■ Sauce can be made 3 days ahead.
■ Storage: Covered, in refrigerator.
■ Freeze: Not suitable.
■ Microwave: Not suitable.

BELOW: From left: Mussels with Garlic Pepper Mayonnaise, Fresh Oysters with Caper Sauce.

Platter, jug, glasses, tablecloth and serviettes from Accoutrement.

LEFT: Mexican Salsa Platter: Clockwise from back: Corn Dip, Salsa, Guacamole.

China from Villeroy & Boch; serviettes and serviette rings from Morris Home & Garden Wares.

PIZZA SHORTBREAD ROUNDS

1 cup (150g) plain flour
2 tablespoons self-raising flour
125g butter, chopped
1 cup (125g) grated tasty
   cheddar cheese
¼ cup (20g) grated parmesan cheese
8 slices mild Danish salami,
   finely chopped
¼ cup (40g) pimiento-stuffed green
   olives, finely chopped
1 tablespoon water, approximately
¾ cup (180ml) sour cream
¼ cup chopped fresh chives

Sift flours into bowl, rub in butter. Stir in cheeses, salami and olives, add enough water to mix to a soft dough. Divide dough into 2 portions, shape each portion into a log 4cm in diameter, wrap in foil, twist ends firmly. Refrigerate until firm.

Cut rolls into 5mm slices, place slices in single layer on oven trays lined with baking paper. Bake, uncovered, in moderate oven about 15 minutes or until lightly browned. Stand biscuits on trays 2 minutes before placing on wire rack to cool. Top each biscuit with ½ teaspoon sour cream, sprinkle with chives.

Makes about 70.

- Biscuits can be made 2 days ahead.
- Storage: Airtight container.
- Freeze: Suitable.
- Microwave: Not suitable.

PARMESAN FISH STRIPS

4 (about 700g) boneless fish fillets
vegetable oil for deep-frying

BATTER
1½ cups (225g) self-raising flour
¾ cup (60g) grated parmesan cheese
¼ cup (60ml) seeded mustard
1¾ cups (430ml) soda water

RED PEPPER MAYONNAISE
1 small red pepper
2 egg yolks
1 tablespoon white vinegar
2 teaspoons tomato paste
¾ teaspoon paprika
1 cup (250ml) vegetable oil

Cut each fillet into about 12 x 8cm lengths. Dip fish in batter, deep-fry in batches in hot oil until browned and cooked through; drain on absorbent paper. Serve hot with red pepper mayonnaise.
Batter: Combine sifted flour, cheese and mustard in large bowl, gradually stir in soda water, stir until smooth; stand, covered, 30 minutes.
Red Pepper Mayonnaise: Quarter pepper, remove seeds and membranes. Grill pepper, skin side up, until skin blackens. Peel and chop pepper. Blend or process egg yolks, vinegar, paste and paprika until smooth. Add oil gradually in a thin stream while motor is operating, blend until thick. Add pepper, blend until smooth.

Makes about 48.

- Red pepper mayonnaise can be made 2 days ahead.
- Storage: Covered, in refrigerator.
- Freeze: Not suitable.
- Microwave: Not suitable.

ABOVE: From left: Parmesan Fish Strips, Pizza Shortbread Rounds.
RIGHT: From left: Spicy Eggplant Fritters with Yogurt Dip, Quick 'n' Easy Artichoke Pizzas.

Above: Large bowl and glasses from Home & Garden; tablecloth and serviettes from Accoutrement.

SPICY EGGPLANT FRITTERS WITH YOGURT DIP

1 large (about 500g) eggplant, peeled, chopped
1 cup (70g) stale breadcrumbs
¾ cup chopped fresh coriander
½ cup (80g) sultanas, chopped
½ cup (125ml) plain yogurt
1 tablespoon tomato paste
3 cloves garlic, crushed
1½ teaspoons ground cumin
1 teaspoon paprika
½ teaspoon ground cardamom
½ teaspoon ground ginger
¼ teaspoon cayenne pepper
½ cup (75g) plain flour
2 eggs, lightly beaten
vegetable oil for deep-frying

YOGURT DIP
1 cup (250ml) plain yogurt
1 tablespoon milk
2 tablespoons chopped fresh mint
2 tablespoons chopped
   fresh coriander
1 teaspoon grated fresh ginger
1 clove garlic, crushed

Steam or microwave eggplant until tender; process eggplant until smooth. Transfer eggplant to bowl, add remaining ingredients except oil; mix well.

Just before serving, drop rounded teaspoons of mixture into hot oil, deep-fry until brown and crisp; drain on absorbent paper.
Yogurt Dip: Combine all ingredients in bowl; mix well.

Serves 10.

■ Eggplant mixture and dip can be prepared 2 days ahead.
■ Storage: Covered, separately, in refrigerator.
■ Freeze: Not suitable.
■ Microwave: Eggplant suitable.

QUICK 'N' EASY ARTICHOKE PIZZAS

2 tablespoons light olive oil
3 medium onions, sliced
2 frozen pizza bases
⅔ cup (160ml) tomato paste
½ cup (60g) grated tasty
   cheddar cheese
½ cup (100g) drained sliced
   sun-dried capsicums
10 artichoke hearts,
   drained, quartered
⅓ cup (55g) pitted black
   olives, quartered
½ cup shredded fresh basil
1½ cups (185g) grated tasty cheddar
   cheese, extra
⅓ cup (25g) grated parmesan cheese

Heat oil in pan, add onions, cook, stirring, until soft; drain on absorbent paper. Spread pizza bases with tomato paste, top with cheddar cheese, onions, capsicums, artichokes, olives, basil, extra cheddar cheese and parmesan cheese. Bake in hot oven about 20 minutes or until bases are crisp and tops lightly browned. Cut into wedges to serve.

Serves 10.

■ Recipe best made close to serving. Onions can be prepared a day ahead.
■ Storage: Covered, in refrigerator.
■ Freeze: Not suitable.
■ Microwave: Not suitable.

POULTRY

In this section, we have used mostly chicken, in dishes so tempting you will find it hard to choose between them. There is a great mix of styles, with terrific casseroles and curries, a tasty lasagne, delicious salads, celebration chicken with walnut pesto, and more. Or, consider a sumptuous turkey roll with cranberry port sauce, and roast quail in lemon marinade.

CHICKEN AND ARTICHOKE SALAD

6 bunches baby beetroot with leaves
2 tablespoons olive oil
2 cloves garlic, crushed
4 large red peppers
½ cup (125ml) olive oil, extra
2 teaspoons lemon pepper seasoning
2 cloves garlic, crushed, extra
8 chicken breast fillets, sliced
8 large drained artichoke
**   hearts, quartered**

TARRAGON DRESSING
½ cup (125ml) olive oil
2 tablespoons lemon juice
2 cloves garlic, crushed
2 tablespoons fresh tarragon leaves

Cut beetroot from leaves, reserve leaves. Boil, steam or microwave beetroot until just tender; drain, peel.

Heat oil in pan, add garlic and beetroot leaves in batches, cook, stirring, about 3 minutes or until leaves are just wilted; drain on absorbent paper.

Quarter peppers, remove seeds and membranes. Grill peppers, skin side up, until skin blisters and blackens. Peel away skin, cut peppers into strips.

Combine extra oil, lemon pepper and extra garlic in bowl, add chicken; mix well. Heat heavy-based pan, add chicken mixture in batches, cook until browned and tender; drain on absorbent paper.

Just before serving, combine beetroot with leaves, peppers, chicken and artichokes in bowl, add tarragon dressing; mix gently.

Tarragon Dressing: Combine all ingredients in jar; shake well.

Serves 10.

- ■ Recipe can be prepared a day ahead.
- ■ Storage: Covered, separately, in refrigerator.
- ■ Freeze: Not suitable.
- ■ Microwave: Beetroot suitable.

RIGHT: Chicken and Artichoke Salad.

CELEBRATION CHICKEN WITH WALNUT PESTO

2kg chicken
8 medium silverbeet leaves
3 medium red peppers
8 slices (about 80g) prosciutto

FILLING
**3 single chicken breast
    fillets, chopped**
1 clove garlic, crushed
1 egg white
⅔ cup (160ml) cream
70g feta cheese
6 pitted black olives, chopped

WALNUT PESTO
**2 cups firmly packed fresh
    basil leaves**
4 cloves garlic, chopped
1 tablespoon fresh rosemary leaves
2 tablespoons fresh thyme leaves
1 cup firmly packed parsley sprigs
½ cup (40g) grated parmesan cheese
**½ cup (60g) chopped
    walnuts, toasted**
2 cups (500ml) olive oil

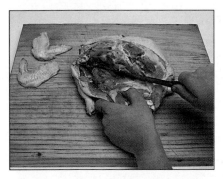

Cut off wing tips at the second joint. Cut through chicken along centre back. Using tip of knife, separate flesh from backbone on 1 side of chicken, cutting through thigh joint, then, following the shape of the bones, gradually ease flesh away from bone. Holding rib cage away from chicken, carefully cut the breast flesh away from the bone, cutting through wing joint.

Hold up 1 thigh with 1 hand. To remove flesh, cut around top of bone, scrape down bone to next joint, cut around flesh again, scrape down to end of leg. Pull bone out and cut away. Repeat boning process with other half of chicken. Turn flesh of thighs and wings inside chicken.

Boil, steam or microwave silverbeet until just tender; drain, rinse under cold water, drain. Quarter peppers, remove seeds and membranes. Grill peppers, skin side up, until skin blisters and blackens. Peel away skin.

Place chicken, skin side down, on bench, cover with prosciutto, silverbeet, then pepper. Spoon filling down centre of chicken. Fold sides over filling, overlapping edges by about 2cm. Sew the overlapping edges together using a needle and thread. Tie chicken with string at 3cm intervals, place on wire rack in baking dish. Bake, uncovered, in moderately hot oven about 1½ hours or until tender; cool. Serve with walnut pesto.

Filling: Blend or process chicken and garlic until smooth, add egg white and cream, process until combined; stir in crumbled cheese and olives.

Walnut Pesto: Blend or process basil, garlic, herbs, cheese and nuts until smooth. Add oil, blend until combined.

Serves 10.

- Recipe can be made a day ahead.
- Storage: Covered, separately, in refrigerator.
- Freeze: Pesto suitable.
- Microwave: Spinach suitable.

CHICKEN CASSEROLE WITH BABY VEGETABLES

2kg chicken thigh fillets
2 tablespoons vegetable oil
2 medium leeks, sliced
2 cloves garlic, crushed
½ cup (125ml) dry white wine
1½ cups (375ml) chicken stock
1 tablespoon chopped fresh thyme
1 tablespoon Dijon mustard
2 bunches (about 550g) baby carrots
750g baby new potatoes
300g sugar snap peas
500g button mushrooms
300ml cream
¼ cup (35g) cornflour
¼ cup (60ml) water

Cut chicken into 3cm pieces. Heat oil in pan, add chicken in batches, cook, stirring, until chicken is browned; remove from pan. Add leeks and garlic to same pan, cook, stirring, until leeks are soft. Stir in wine, bring to boil. Stir in chicken, stock, thyme and mustard, simmer, covered, about 20 minutes or until chicken is cooked through.

Boil, steam or microwave carrots, potatoes and peas separately until tender. Add cooked vegetables, mushrooms, cream and blended cornflour and water to chicken in pan, stir over heat until mixture boils and thickens.

Serves 10.

■ Recipe can be made a day ahead.
■ Storage: Covered, in refrigerator.
■ Freeze: Not suitable.
■ Microwave: Carrots, potatoes and peas suitable.

LEFT: Celebration Chicken with Walnut Pesto.
ABOVE: Chicken Casserole with Baby Vegetables.

Above: China from Waterford Wedgwood; cutlery and glasses from The Bay Tree Kitchen Shop.

ROAST QUAIL WITH POTATOES AND PANCETTA

Butterfly quail by cutting each side of backbone and removing backbone.

10 quail, butterflied
4 large potatoes, sliced
80g butter, melted
3 medium red Spanish onions, sliced
100g sliced pancetta, chopped
2 cloves garlic, crushed
1 tablespoon chopped fresh thyme
1 tablespoon chopped fresh oregano

MARINADE
2 medium lemons
¼ cup (60ml) lemon juice
½ cup (125ml) olive oil

LEMON GARLIC SAUCE
300ml thickened cream
2 cloves garlic, crushed
2 teaspoons lemon juice
60g butter, chopped
1 teaspoon chopped fresh thyme

Place quail in dish, add marinade, cover, refrigerate 3 hours or overnight.

Combine potatoes with remaining ingredients in large baking dish. Bake, uncovered, in very hot oven about 45 minutes or until potatoes are tender.

Drain quail, reserve marinade. Place quail on wire racks in baking dishes, bake, uncovered, in hot oven about 25 minutes or until tender; brush occasionally with reserved marinade. Serve with potato mixture and sauce.

Marinade: Peel rind thinly, cut into thin strips. Combine with remaining ingredients in bowl; mix well.

Lemon Garlic Sauce: Combine cream, garlic and juice in pan, simmer, uncovered, about 5 minutes or until reduced by a third. Gradually whisk in butter, whisk until thickened slightly; stir in thyme.

Serves 10.

- Quail can be prepared a day ahead.
- Storage: Covered, in refrigerator.
- Freeze: Marinated quail suitable.
- Microwave: Not suitable.

MARINATED CHICKEN WITH PECAN BUTTER

10 chicken breast fillets
3 cloves garlic, crushed
⅓ cup chopped fresh basil
½ cup (125ml) dry white wine
⅔ cup (160ml) olive oil
2 tablespoons lemon juice

PECAN BUTTER
20g butter
½ small onion, finely chopped
⅓ cup (40g) pecans, toasted, chopped
1 tablespoon grated orange rind
230g soft butter, extra
1 tablespoon orange juice

VEGETABLE SALAD
2 bunches (about 500g) fresh asparagus
200g green beans
150g yellow squash, quartered
1 butter lettuce
1 red coral lettuce
1 medium orange, segmented

DRESSING
1 teaspoon Dijon mustard
¼ cup (60ml) balsamic vinegar
⅔ cup (160ml) extra virgin olive oil

Gently pound chicken to even thickness, using a meat mallet. Combine garlic, basil, wine, oil and juice in large bowl, add chicken, stir to coat with marinade; cover, refrigerate several hours or overnight.

Drain chicken from marinade, discard marinade. Cook chicken in batches on heated griddle pan or barbecue until browned and tender. Serve with vegetable salad, top with pecan butter.

Pecan Butter: Heat butter in pan, add onion, nuts and rind, cook, stirring, until onion is soft; cool. Combine onion mixture, extra butter and juice in bowl; mix well. Spoon mixture onto sheet of foil, shape into 14cm log, roll up firmly, twisting ends of foil. Refrigerate until firm.

Vegetable Salad: Boil, steam or microwave asparagus, beans and squash separately until just tender; drain, rinse under cold water, drain well. Combine vegetables, torn lettuce leaves, orange segments and dressing in bowl; mix gently.

Dressing: Combine all ingredients in jar; shake well.

Serves 10.

- Chicken and pecan butter can be prepared a day ahead.
- Storage: Covered, separately, in refrigerator.
- Freeze: Uncooked, marinated chicken and pecan butter suitable.
- Microwave: Vegetables suitable.

LEFT: Roast Quail with Potatoes and Pancetta.
ABOVE: Marinated Chicken with Pecan Butter.

Left: China and glasses from Waterford Wedgwood; cutlery from The Bay Tree Kitchen Shop. Above: China and napery from Home & Garden on the Mall.

TURKEY ROLL WITH CRANBERRY PORT SAUCE

3.6kg turkey
30g butter, melted
¼ cup (35g) plain flour
2¼ cups (560ml) chicken stock
⅔ cup (160ml) port
½ cup (125ml) cranberry sauce

SEASONING
2 tablespoons vegetable oil
3 bacon rashers, chopped
2 medium onions, chopped
500g minced chicken
2 cups (140g) stale breadcrumbs
⅓ cup (50g) chopped pistachios
⅓ cup (50g) chopped dried apricots
⅓ cup (70g) chopped pitted prunes
¼ cup chopped fresh sage
1 tablespoon chopped fresh thyme
1 egg, lightly beaten

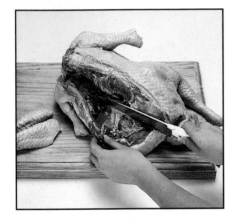

Cut off wing tips at the second joint. Cut through turkey along centre back. Using tip of knife, separate flesh from backbone on 1 side of turkey, cutting through thigh joint, then, following the shape of the bones, gradually ease flesh away from bone. Holding rib cage away from turkey, carefully cut the breast flesh away from the bone, cutting through wing joint.

Hold up 1 thigh with 1 hand. To remove flesh, cut around top of bone, scrape down bone to next joint, cut around flesh again, scrape down to end of leg. Pull bone out and cut away. Repeat boning process with other half of turkey. Turn flesh of thighs and wings inside turkey.

Place turkey, skin side down, on bench; pound lightly to even thickness, using a meat mallet. Spread seasoning over turkey, roll up from long side, secure with skewers. Cut roll in half, secure rolls with string at 2cm intervals, remove skewers.

Place rolls on wire rack in baking dish, add ½ cup (125ml) water to dish. Brush rolls with half the butter, bake, uncovered, in moderate oven about 1¼ hours or until tender. Brush with remaining butter during cooking. Remove rolls and rack from dish, stand 10 minutes.

Drain juices from dish, reserve ¼ cup (60ml) juices. Heat juices in dish, add flour, cook, stirring, until lightly browned. Remove from heat, gradually stir in stock and port, stir over heat until sauce boils and thickens. Strain sauce, return to clean pan, add cranberry sauce, stir until hot. Serve cranberry port sauce with turkey.

Seasoning: Heat oil in pan, add bacon and onions, cook, stirring, until onions are soft. Combine onion mixture with remaining ingredients in bowl; mix well.

Serves 10 to 12.

■ Recipe can be made a day ahead.
■ Storage: Covered, separately, in refrigerator.
■ Freeze: Uncooked turkey rolls suitable.
■ Microwave: Not suitable.

LEFT: Turkey Roll with Cranberry Port Sauce.
ABOVE: Chicken Nicoise Salad.

Left: China and tray from Corso de Fiori. Above: Platter from Accoutrement.

CHICKEN NICOISE SALAD

10 chicken breast fillets
2 tablespoons seasoned pepper
2 tablespoons vegetable oil
500g baby new potatoes, halved
200g green beans, halved
1 large cos lettuce
250g cherry tomatoes, halved
1 cup (160g) pitted black olives, halved
4 hard-boiled eggs, quartered

DRESSING
¾ cup (180ml) olive oil
¼ cup (60ml) tarragon vinegar
1½ teaspoons French mustard
1 teaspoon sugar

Flatten chicken gently using a meat mallet; sprinkle with seasoned pepper. Heat oil in pan, add chicken in batches, cook until browned and tender; drain on absorbent paper, cool. Cut chicken into 2cm strips. Boil, steam or microwave potatoes and beans separately until tender; drain, rinse under cold water, drain.

Reserve 8 of the outside lettuce leaves. Combine remaining torn leaves, chicken, potatoes, beans, tomatoes and olives with dressing in large bowl; mix gently. Line serving bowl with reserved leaves, add chicken mixture, top with eggs.

Dressing: Combine all ingredients in jar; shake well.

Serves 10.

■ Recipe can be prepared a day ahead.
■ Storage: Covered, separately, in refrigerator.
■ Freeze: Not suitable.
■ Microwave: Potatoes and beans suitable.

CHICKEN AND LENTIL CURRY

½ cup (100g) dried chick peas
2 medium onions, chopped
6 cloves garlic
8cm piece (about 60g) fresh ginger
¼ cup chopped fresh mint
½ cup chopped fresh coriander
½ teaspoon sambal oelek
20g ghee
20 (about 3.6kg) chicken pieces
¼ cup (30g) curry powder
1 tablespoon ground cumin
1 teaspoon ground cardamom
3 cups (750ml) chicken stock
1 litre (4 cups) water
3 medium tomatoes, chopped
300g pumpkin, chopped
1 large potato, chopped
¾ cup (150g) red lentils
⅓ bunch (about 220g)
    English spinach

Place chick peas in bowl; cover well with water, cover, stand overnight.

Process onions, garlic, ginger, herbs and sambal oelek until finely minced. Heat ghee in pan, add chicken in batches, cook, turning, until browned; drain chicken on absorbent paper.

Drain all but 2 tablespoons juices from pan. Add onion mixture to pan, cook, stirring, 2 minutes. Add spices, cook, stirring, until fragrant. Stir in drained chick peas, stock, water, tomatoes, pumpkin, potato, and lentils, simmer, uncovered, 20 minutes. Add chicken, simmer, covered, further 30 minutes or until chicken and vegetables are tender. Add spinach, simmer, uncovered, further 5 minutes. Remove chicken from sauce, blend or process sauce until smooth. Return sauce and chicken to pan, cook until heated through.

Serves 10.

- Recipe can be made 2 days ahead.
- Storage: Covered, in refrigerator.
- Freeze: Suitable.
- Microwave: Not suitable.

HOI SIN CHICKEN AND EGG NOODLE SALAD

⅔ cup (160ml) hoi sin sauce
2 tablespoons mild sweet chilli sauce
4 cloves garlic, crushed
⅓ cup (80ml) dry sherry
8 chicken breast fillets, thinly sliced
2 tablespoons vegetable oil
375g packet fresh egg noodles
300g sugar snap peas
2 medium carrots
2 medium red peppers
2 cups (300g) unsalted
    roasted cashews
2 cups (160g) bean sprouts
1 small Chinese cabbage,
    thinly shredded
8 green shallots, chopped
½ cup chopped fresh coriander

DRESSING
¼ cup (60ml) lemon juice
¼ cup (60ml) sesame oil
½ cup (125ml) light soy sauce
2 tablespoons sugar
¼ cup (60ml) light olive oil

Combine sauces, garlic and sherry in bowl, add chicken; mix well. Cover, refrigerate 1 hour.

Heat oil in pan, add undrained chicken in batches, cook until browned and tender; drain on absorbent paper. Add noodles to large pan of boiling water, boil, uncovered, until just tender; drain, rinse under cold water, drain. Boil, steam or microwave peas until just tender; drain, rinse under cold water, drain. Cut carrots and peppers into thin strips.

Just before serving, combine chicken, noodles, peas, carrots and peppers with remaining ingredients in bowl, add dressing; mix gently.

Dressing: Combine all ingredients in jar; shake well.

Serves 10 to 12.

- Chicken and dressing can be prepared a day ahead.
- Storage: Covered, separately, in refrigerator.
- Freeze: Not suitable.
- Microwave: Noodles and peas suitable.

ABOVE: Chicken and Lentil Curry.
RIGHT: Hoi Sin Chicken and Egg Noodle Salad.

CHICKEN AND SPINACH ROULADE

500g frozen spinach, thawed, drained
125g butter, chopped
⅔ cup (100g) plain flour
2 cups (500ml) milk
8 eggs, separated
½ cup chopped fresh parsley
⅓ cup chopped fresh basil

CHICKEN FILLING
40g butter
¼ cup (35g) plain flour
1½ cups (375ml) milk
1 cup (250ml) cream
2 tablespoons lime juice
300ml sour cream
2 teaspoons prepared horseradish
⅓ cup (25g) grated parmesan cheese
3 cups (450g) chopped
    cooked chicken
1 cup (135g) drained chopped
    sun-dried tomatoes
8 green shallots, chopped
½ cup chopped fresh basil

Grease 2 x 26cm x 32cm Swiss roll pans, line base and sides with baking paper. Place spinach in dry pan, cook, stirring, until liquid is evaporated.

Melt butter in pan, add flour, stir until bubbling. Remove pan from heat, gradually stir in milk, stir over heat until mixture boils and thickens. Transfer mixture to large bowl, stir in spinach, egg yolks and herbs.

Beat egg whites in large bowl with electric mixer until firm peaks form, fold into spinach mixture in 2 batches. Divide mixture between prepared pans. Bake in hot oven about 12 minutes or until puffed and browned. Turn onto wire racks

covered with tea-towels, remove paper, roll each tightly in a tea-towel, stand 3 minutes, unroll, stand 5 minutes.

Divide chicken filling evenly between roulades, roll up tightly. Cover, refrigerate until firm.

Chicken Filling: Melt butter in pan, add flour, stir until bubbling. Remove from heat, gradually stir in combined milk and cream. Stir over heat until mixture boils and thickens. Stir in remaining ingredients, cool.

Serves 10.

- ▓ Recipe can be made a day ahead.
- ▓ Storage: Covered, in refrigerator.
- ▓ Freeze: Not suitable.
- ▓ Microwave: Not suitable.

HERB-CRUMBED CHICKEN WITH CREAM SAUCE

20 chicken thigh fillets
plain flour
4 eggs, lightly beaten
3½ cups (245g) stale white
   breadcrumbs
1½ tablespoons chopped
   fresh oregano
¼ cup chopped fresh chives
150g ghee

CREAM SAUCE
30g butter
1 small onion, finely chopped
½ cup (125ml) dry white wine
pinch saffron powder
1 teaspoon chicken stock powder
300ml cream
2 teaspoons cornflour
¾ cup (180ml) milk
1 small tomato, peeled,
   seeded, chopped

Toss chicken in flour, shake away excess flour, dip in eggs, then combined breadcrumbs, oregano and chives; cover, refrigerate 15 minutes.

Heat half the ghee in large pan, add half the chicken in batches, cook on both sides until browned and cooked through; drain on absorbent paper. Repeat with remaining ghee and chicken. Serve chicken with cream sauce.

Cream Sauce: Heat butter in pan, add onion, cook, stirring, until soft. Add wine and saffron, simmer, uncovered, about 5 minutes or until reduced by half. Add stock powder, cream and blended cornflour and milk, cook, stirring, until mixture boils and thickens; stir in tomato.

Serves 10.

- ▓ Chicken and sauce can be prepared a day ahead.
- ▓ Storage: Covered, separately, in refrigerator.
- ▓ Freeze: Uncooked, crumbed chicken suitable.
- ▓ Microwave: Sauce suitable.

LEFT: Herb-Crumbed Chicken with Cream Sauce.
ABOVE: Chicken and Spinach Roulade.

Left: China and napery from Home & Garden on the Mall. Above: China and glassware from Home & Garden on the Mall.

SEAFOOD

As soon as you look at our tempting seafood recipes, you will see they are oceans ahead in style, flavour, and variety. In them, we have come up with the freshest, most tempting combinations imaginable, making them top favourites as main meals both elegant and homely, or as part of a buffet. For example, the centrepiece of your buffet could be a whole, baked snapper with black bean sauce, or a lovely seafood platter. Yet other ideas would be a sizzling success on the barbecue.

BARBECUED FISH WITH SALSA AND AVOCADO SAUCE

10 firm white fish cutlets
⅓ cup (80ml) olive oil

AVOCADO SAUCE
1 large avocado, chopped
1 egg yolk
¼ cup (60ml) lime juice
2 cloves garlic, crushed
½ teaspoon sugar
1 cup (250ml) olive oil

SALSA
1 medium green pepper
2 medium tomatoes, finely chopped
310g can corn kernels, drained
1 medium red Spanish onion, finely chopped
2 tablespoons chopped fresh coriander
2 tablespoons mild sweet chilli sauce

Brush fish with oil, barbecue or grill fish until just tender. Serve hot or cold with salsa and avocado sauce.

Avocado Sauce: Blend or process avocado, egg yolk, juice, garlic and sugar until smooth. Add oil gradually in a thin stream while motor is operating; blend until thick.

Salsa: Quarter pepper, remove seeds and membranes. Grill pepper, skin side up, until skin blisters and blackens. Peel away skin, chop pepper finely. Combine pepper and remaining ingredients in bowl; mix well.

Serves 10.

- Recipe can be made a day ahead.
- Storage: Covered, separately, in refrigerator.
- Freeze: Not suitable.
- Microwave: Not suitable.

RIGHT: Barbecued Fish with Salsa and Avocado Sauce.

Plate, bowl and fabric from Accoutrement; glasses, gold pumpkin, serviettes and serviette rings from Home & Garden on the Mall.

BRIOCHE ROLLS WITH CREAMY TROUT FILLING

1 tablespoon (14g) dried yeast
1 teaspoon sugar
¾ cup (180ml) warm milk
3 cups (450g) plain flour
2 eggs, lightly beaten
90g butter, chopped
1 egg, lightly beaten, extra
1 tablespoon sesame seeds
2 teaspoons poppy seeds
1 teaspoon cumin seeds
2 teaspoons sea salt

FILLING
1kg ocean trout fillets
40g butter
2 medium onions, chopped
2 cloves garlic, crushed
⅓ cup (80ml) sour cream
5 hard-boiled eggs, quartered
1 tablespoon Dijon mustard
1 cup (150g) pimiento-stuffed
    green olives
¼ cup chopped fresh chives
1 tablespoon chopped fresh oregano
½ cup (65g) drained chopped
    sun-dried tomatoes

Combine yeast with sugar in bowl, add milk, stir until well combined; cover, stand in warm place about 10 minutes or until mixture is frothy.

Sift flour into bowl, stir in combined eggs and yeast mixture. Turn dough onto lightly floured surface, knead about 5 minutes or until dough is smooth and elastic. Gradually knead in small pieces of soft butter, knead until smooth. Place dough in oiled bowl; cover, stand in warm place about 40 minutes or until doubled in size.

Turn dough onto floured surface, knead until smooth; divide into 2 portions. Roll each portion into 24cm x 34cm rectangle. Place half the filling along centre of each rectangle, brush edges of dough with some of the beaten extra egg. Fold sides and ends over filling, pinch seams firmly to seal. Place rolls, seam side down, on greased oven trays, brush with more remaining extra egg, sprinkle with combined seeds and salt. Bake in moderately hot oven about 20 minutes or until browned and heated through.

Filling: Poach, steam or microwave trout until tender; cool. Remove skin and bones from trout, flake into 3cm pieces. Heat butter in pan, add onions and garlic, cook, stirring, until onions are soft. Combine trout and onion mixture with remaining ingredients in bowl; mix lightly to combine.

Makes 2.

- Recipe can be made a day ahead.
- Storage: Covered, in refrigerator.
- Freeze: Not suitable.
- Microwave: Filling suitable.

BELOW: Brioche Rolls with Creamy Trout Filling.

Plates, serviettes and tray from Accoutrement; glasses and vase from Morris Home & Garden Wares.

SMOKED SALMON AND RICE SLICE

1⅓ cups (265g) white rice
400g smoked salmon, chopped
16 eggs
1 cup (80g) grated parmesan cheese
2 teaspoons cracked black pepper
1 tablespoon chopped fresh thyme
300ml sour cream
1 tablespoon French mustard
4 sheets fillo pastry
50g butter, melted
1 teaspoon poppy seeds

HERB MAYONNAISE
1 cup (250ml) mayonnaise
½ cup (125ml) sour cream
2 tablespoons milk
1 tablespoon French mustard
¼ cup chopped fresh parsley
2 teaspoons chopped fresh thyme
2 tablespoons chopped fresh basil

Grease 2 x 23cm square slab cake pans, line bases and sides with baking paper, grease paper. Add rice to pan of boiling water, boil, uncovered, until just tender; drain, cool. Press rice evenly over bases of prepared pans.

Combine salmon, eggs, cheese, pepper, thyme, sour cream and mustard in large bowl; mix well. Pour egg mixture evenly over rice in pans. Layer 2 sheets of pastry together, brushing each sheet with butter, fold in half, trim to fit top of 1 pan. Place pastry over salmon mixture; brush with butter, sprinkle with half the seeds. Repeat with remaining pastry, butter and seeds. Bake, uncovered, in moderate oven about 40 minutes or until set and lightly browned (change position of pans halfway through cooking). Stand 5 minutes before cutting. Serve hot or cold with herb mayonnaise.

Herb Mayonnaise: Combine all ingredients in bowl; mix well.

Serves 10.

- Recipe can be made 3 hours ahead.
- Storage: Covered, separately, in refrigerator.
- Freeze: Not suitable.
- Microwave: Rice suitable.

LEFT: Smoked Salmon and Rice Slice.

BAKED PUMPKIN GNOCCHI WITH SEAFOOD SAUCE

You will need to cook about 2.5kg pumpkin for this recipe.

500g small calamari tubes
2kg cooked medium prawns
1kg small mussels
2 cups (500ml) water
40g butter
4 cloves garlic, crushed
2 cups (500ml) dry white wine
2 cups (500ml) fish stock
300ml cream
2 tablespoons cornflour
2 tablespoons water, extra
300ml sour cream
1 cup (80g) grated parmesan cheese
¼ cup chopped fresh basil
2 tablespoons chopped fresh dill
2 tablespoons chopped fresh chives

BAKED PUMPKIN GNOCCHI
6 cups (about 1.5kg) cooked
　　mashed pumpkin
180g butter, melted
1½ cups (240g) semolina
1 cup (80g) grated parmesan cheese
2 cloves garlic, crushed
8 eggs, lightly beaten

Cut calamari into rings. Shell and devein prawns, leaving tails intact. Scrub mussels, remove beards. Heat water in large pan, add mussels, cook, covered, over high heat about 5 minutes or until mussels open. Drain mussels; discard liquid.

Heat butter in pan, add garlic, cook, stirring, until fragrant. Add wine, bring to boil. Add stock, cream and blended cornflour and extra water, cook, stirring, until mixture boils and thickens slightly. Stir in calamari, simmer, uncovered, about 1 minute or until just tender.

Just before serving, stir in sour cream, cheese, herbs, prawns and mussels; stir until hot (do not boil). Serve seafood sauce over baked pumpkin gnocchi.

Baked Pumpkin Gnocchi: Grease 2 x 20cm x 30cm lamington pans; line pans with baking paper to cover base and extend over 2 opposite sides. Combine all ingredients in large bowl; mix well. Spread mixture into prepared pans, bake in moderately hot oven about 30 minutes or until set. Turn gnocchi onto board, cut into 3cm x 5cm pieces.

Serves 10.

■ Gnocchi can be made and cut into pieces a day ahead. Place on oven trays, loosely covered with foil, in moderate oven to reheat. Sauce can be prepared a day ahead.
■ Storage: Covered, separately, in refrigerator.
■ Freeze: Gnocchi suitable.
■ Microwave: Not suitable.

SEAFOOD PAELLA

500g medium cooked prawns
20 large mussels
2 (about 400g) lobster tails
500g calamari tubes
¼ cup (60ml) olive oil
3 cloves garlic, crushed
8 green shallots, chopped
1 medium red pepper, chopped
2 medium green peppers, chopped
810g can tomatoes
1 teaspoon sugar
2 teaspoons paprika
3½ cups (700g) long-grain rice
1.25 litres (5 cups) water
¼ teaspoon ground saffron
2 teaspoons chicken stock powder
500g white fish fillets, chopped
300g button mushrooms, quartered
½ cup chopped fresh parsley

Shell and devein prawns, leaving tails intact. Scrub mussels, remove beards. Cut lobster into 1cm medallions. Cut calamari into 3cm x 6cm lengths, score shallow diagonal slashes in criss-cross pattern on inside surface. Heat oil in large pan, add garlic, shallots and peppers, cook, stirring, 3 minutes. Stir in undrained crushed tomatoes, sugar and paprika, simmer, stirring, about 3 minutes or until slightly thickened.

Stir in rice, water, saffron and stock powder, stir until boiling, then simmer, covered, 10 minutes. Stir in mussels, top with lobster, calamari, fish and mushrooms, simmer, covered, about 5 minutes, or until seafood is tender. Add prawns and parsley, stir gently until heated through.

Serves 10.

■ Recipe best made close to serving.
■ Freeze: Not suitable.
■ Microwave: Not suitable.

LEFT: Baked Pumpkin Gnocchi with Seafood Sauce.
ABOVE: Seafood Paella.

Left: China from Villa Italiana. Above: Platter from Villa Italiana; tiles from Country Floors.

FRESH TUNA AND PASTA SALAD

⅓ cup (80ml) olive oil
50g butter
6 medium onions, sliced
4 cloves garlic, crushed
⅓ cup (80ml) red wine vinegar
2 tablespoons chopped fresh thyme
1 tablespoon sugar
1kg tuna steaks
½ cup (125ml) olive oil, extra
2 tablespoons red wine vinegar, extra
1kg penne pasta
250g cherry tomatoes, halved
1 bunch (about 650g) English
    spinach, shredded

Heat oil and butter in heavy-based pan, add onions and garlic, cook, covered, stirring occasionally, about 30 minutes or until onions are very soft. Add vinegar, thyme and sugar, simmer, uncovered, 1 minute.

Add tuna to onion mixture, cook, uncovered, until tuna is cooked as desired. Remove tuna from pan, cut into bite-sized pieces. Add extra oil and extra vinegar to onion mixture, stir until combined.

Meanwhile, add pasta to large pan of boiling water, boil, uncovered, until just tender; drain. Combine onion mixture, pasta, tomatoes and spinach in large bowl; mix well. Add tuna; mix gently.

Serves 10.

- ■ Recipe best made close to serving.
- ■ Freeze: Not suitable.
- ■ Microwave: Pasta suitable.

COCONUT SEAFOOD CURRY

500g boneless fish fillets
1.5kg medium uncooked prawns
500g calamari tubes
60g butter
3 medium onions, chopped
4 cloves garlic, sliced
1 tablespoon grated fresh ginger
3 teaspoons ground cumin
3 teaspoons ground coriander
¾ teaspoon turmeric
1 cinnamon stick
3 teaspoons black mustard seeds
1 teaspoon sambal oelek
4 x 283ml cans coconut cream
2 tablespoons plain flour
2 cups (500ml) water

Cut fish into 3cm pieces. Shell and devein prawns, leaving tails intact. Cut calamari tubes in half, score shallow diagonal slashes in criss-cross pattern on inside of calamari. Cut calamari into 4cm pieces.

Heat butter in large pan, add onions, garlic, ginger, spices, mustard seeds and sambal oelek, cook, stirring, until onions are soft. Stir in coconut cream and blended flour and water, stir over heat until mixture boils and thickens.

Just before serving, add seafood, simmer, uncovered, about 5 minutes or until seafood is just tender; discard cinnamon.

Serves 10.

- ■ Recipe, without seafood, can be prepared a day ahead.
- ■ Storage: Covered, in refrigerator.
- ■ Freeze: Not suitable.
- ■ Microwave: Suitable.

SPICY CAJUN KEBABS WITH PINEAPPLE SALSA

1kg (about 20) large uncooked prawns
1kg firm white fish fillets
750g salmon fillets
1 medium red pepper
40 large scallops

MARINADE
2 tablespoons Worcestershire sauce
1½ tablespoons paprika
1 tablespoon ground black pepper
1 tablespoon dry mustard
1½ teaspoons salt
1 teaspoon onion powder
¼ teaspoon tabasco sauce
¼ teaspoon cayenne pepper
5 cloves garlic, crushed
¼ cup (60ml) lemon juice
1½ cups (375ml) beer

PINEAPPLE SALSA
½ medium pineapple, chopped
½ medium yellow pepper, finely chopped
½ small onion, finely chopped
⅓ cup chopped fresh mint
1 tablespoon chopped fresh coriander

Shell and devein prawns, leaving tails intact. Cut fish fillets into 3cm pieces. Cut pepper into 4cm squares, then in half diagonally to make triangles.

Thread seafood and peppers evenly onto 10 skewers, place kebabs in single layer in shallow dishes, pour over marinade. Cover, refrigerate several hours or overnight; turn occasionally.

Remove kebabs from marinade, discard marinade. Place kebabs in single layer in 2 baking dishes, bake, covered, in hot oven about 15 minutes or until seafood is cooked (or, grill or barbecue). Serve kebabs with pineapple salsa.

Marinade: Combine all ingredients in bowl; mix well.

Pineapple Salsa: Process pineapple until roughly chopped; stir in remaining ingredients.

Serves 10.

- Kebabs and salsa can be prepared a day ahead.
- Storage: Covered, separately, in refrigerator.
- Freeze: Not suitable.
- Microwave: Suitable.

LEFT: Coconut Seafood Curry.
BELOW LEFT: Fresh Tuna and Pasta Salad.
BELOW: Spicy Cajun Kebabs with Pineapple Salsa.

Left: Plates and serviettes from Accoutrement.
Below left: Bowl and serviettes from Accoutrement.
Below: Serving dish and tiles from Country Floors.

BAKED SNAPPER WITH BLACK BEAN SAUCE

2.3kg whole snapper
1 tablespoon vegetable oil
1 tablespoon mild sweet chilli sauce
3 green shallots, chopped
2 tablespoons fresh coriander leaves

BLACK BEAN SAUCE
50g Chinese dried mushrooms, halved
1 tablespoon vegetable oil
2 medium onions, sliced
2 cloves garlic, sliced
390g can pimientos, drained, sliced
⅓ cup (80ml) black bean sauce
2 teaspoons brown sugar
½ cup (125ml) sweet sherry
¾ cup (180ml) water

Place snapper in large baking dish, brush with combined oil and chilli sauce; cover tail and fins with foil. Bake, uncovered, in moderate oven about 35 minutes. Serve topped with black bean sauce; sprinkle with shallots and coriander.

Black Bean Sauce: Place mushrooms in heatproof bowl, cover with boiling water, stand 10 minutes. Drain mushrooms. Heat oil in pan, add onions and garlic, cook, stirring, until onions are soft. Add mushrooms, pimientos, sauce, sugar, sherry and water, simmer, uncovered, about 10 minutes or until black bean sauce is thickened.

Serves 10 as part of a buffet.

- Black bean sauce can be made a day ahead.
- Storage: Covered, in refrigerator.
- Freeze: Not suitable.
- Microwave: Not suitable.

SALMON CREPE CAKES

125g butter
12 green shallots, chopped
500g button mushrooms, sliced
4 cloves garlic, crushed
½ cup (75g) plain flour
3¼ cups (810ml) milk
300ml cream
2 x 415g cans salmon, drained, flaked
¼ cup (60ml) tomato paste
⅓ cup chopped fresh dill
½ cup (40g) grated parmesan cheese
½ cup (60g) grated tasty cheddar cheese

CREPES
2 cups (300g) plain flour
7 eggs, lightly beaten
2 tablespoons vegetable oil
3 cups (750ml) milk
20g butter

Lightly grease 2 x 20cm springform tins. Heat butter in pan, add shallots, mushrooms and garlic, cook, stirring, until mushrooms are lightly browned. Add flour, cook, stirring, until mixture is dry and grainy. Remove from heat, gradually stir in milk and cream. Stir over heat until mixture boils and thickens; stir in salmon, paste and dill.

Place a crepe in base of each prepared tin, spread with 1/3 cup (80ml) salmon filling. Repeat layering crepes and filling, ending with filling, sprinkle with combined cheeses. Place tins on oven trays, bake, uncovered, in moderate oven about 40 minutes or until heated through. Stand 10 minutes, remove rings; cut cakes into wedges to serve.

Crepes: Sift flour into large bowl, gradually whisk in combined eggs, oil and milk; whisk until smooth. (Or, blend or process all ingredients until smooth.) Strain batter through fine sieve. Heat a small amount of butter in 18cm crepe pan, pour 1/4 cup (60ml) batter into pan, cook until lightly browned underneath. Turn crepe, brown other side. Repeat with remaining batter. You will need 20 crepes for this recipe.

Serves 10 to 12.

- Recipe can be made a day ahead.
- Storage: Covered, in refrigerator.
- Freeze: Crepes suitable.
- Microwave: Not suitable.

LEFT: Baked Snapper with Black Bean Sauce.
ABOVE: Salmon Crepe Cakes.
RIGHT: Barbecued Fish with Pepper Salad.

Left: Platter and plates from Accoutrement; tablecloth, glasses, basket and serviette rings from Home & Garden on the Mall. Above: Plates, glasses, tablecloth, serviettes and serviette rings from Accoutrement. Right: Pottery from Kenwick Galleries; basket from The Melbourne Shop.

BARBECUED FISH WITH PEPPER SALAD

You need about 5 limes for this recipe.

2kg firm white fish fillets
3/4 cup (180ml) olive oil
1 tablespoon grated lime rind
3/4 cup (180ml) lime juice
2 cloves garlic, crushed
2 teaspoons seeded mustard
1 teaspoon brown sugar
2 medium red peppers, sliced
2 medium green peppers, sliced
2 medium yellow peppers, sliced
3/4 cup chopped fresh parsley
1/3 cup (50g) pine nuts, toasted

Cut fish into 1.5cm strips. Combine fish, oil, rind, juice, garlic, mustard and sugar in bowl; mix gently, cover, refrigerate 1 hour.

Combine peppers and half the parsley in bowl; mix well. Place pepper mixture on large plate. Remove fish from marinade; reserve marinade. Barbecue or grill fish in batches until tender, place fish on pepper mixture, sprinkle fish with nuts and remaining parsley.

Place reserved marinade in small pan, simmer, uncovered, 1 minute. Pour marinade over fish.

Serves 10.

- Recipe must be prepared an hour ahead.
- Storage: Covered, in refrigerator.
- Freeze: Not suitable.
- Microwave: Not suitable.

SEAFOOD PLATTER

750g thick white fish fillets
1 tablespoon olive oil
⅓ cup (80ml) light soy sauce
2 tablespoons mild sweet chilli sauce
1 teaspoon grated fresh ginger
¼ teaspoon five spice powder
1 teaspoon sesame oil
1kg medium cooked prawns
12 oysters
1 cup (about 50g) firmly packed
    watercress sprigs
4 limes, quartered

LEMON HERB CALAMARI
1kg calamari tubes
2 tablespoons olive oil
3 cloves garlic, crushed
2 teaspoons grated lemon rind
2 tablespoons chopped fresh parsley
¼ cup (60ml) olive oil, extra

CRISP BAKED SARDINES
10 fresh sardines
2 tablespoons grated
    parmesan cheese
2 tablespoons stale breadcrumbs
2 tablespoons olive oil

AOLI
2 egg yolks
2 teaspoons white vinegar
4 cloves garlic, crushed
1½ cups (375ml) olive oil
2 tablespoons milk, approximately

Cut fish into 3cm pieces. Heat olive oil in pan, add fish in batches, cook over high heat until lightly browned and cooked through. Place fish in large bowl, add combined sauces, ginger, five spice powder and sesame oil; cover, refrigerate several hours or overnight.

Drain fish, discard marinade. Shell and devein prawns, leaving tails intact. Place fish, prawns, oysters, lemon herb calamari, crisp baked sardines and watercress on platter; serve with aoli and lime wedges.

Lemon Herb Calamari: Cut calamari tubes in half, score shallow diagonal slashes in criss-cross pattern inside calamari. Cut calamari into 4cm x 6cm pieces. Heat oil in pan, add calamari in batches, cook over high heat for few minutes, or until lightly browned and tender. Combine hot calamari with garlic, rind, parsley and extra oil; cool. Cover, refrigerate 3 hours or overnight.

Crisp Baked Sardines: Remove entrails from sardines, place sardines in single layer on greased oven tray. Sprinkle sardines with combined cheese and breadcrumbs; drizzle with oil. Bake, uncovered, in hot oven about 10 minutes or until sardines are browned and tender.

Aoli: Process yolks, vinegar and garlic until smooth. Gradually add oil in a thin stream while motor is operating; process until thick. Add enough milk to give desired consistency.

Serves 10.

- Fish, calamari and aoli can be prepared a day ahead.
- Storage: Covered, separately, in refrigerator.
- Freeze: Not suitable.
- Microwave: Not suitable.

LEFT: Seafood Platter.
ABOVE: Thai-Style Prawn and Scallop Salad.

Left: Silverware and glass from The Bay Tree Kitchen Shop. Above: Bowls from Accoutrement; tray from Home & Garden on the Mall.

THAI-STYLE PRAWN AND SCALLOP SALAD

8 green shallots
2 tablespoons vegetable oil
3 cloves garlic, crushed
1 medium red pepper, thinly sliced
1 medium yellow pepper, thinly sliced
2 bunches (about 1.2kg) bok choy
2kg medium uncooked prawns
1 tablespoon vegetable oil, extra
1kg scallops
1kg fresh (no cook) rice noodles

DRESSING
¼ cup (60ml) mild sweet chilli sauce
½ cup (125ml) lime juice
1 tablespoon fish sauce
1 tablespoon chopped fresh
    lemon grass
¼ cup chopped fresh coriander
½ cup chopped fresh mint

Cut shallots diagonally into 3cm lengths. Heat oil in pan, add shallots, garlic and peppers, cook, stirring, until shallots are just tender; remove from pan. Remove and discard stalks from bok choy. Tear leaves in half, add to pan or wok in batches, cook, stirring, until just wilted; remove from pan.

Shell and devein prawns, leaving tails intact. Heat extra oil in pan, add prawns and scallops in batches, cook until tender; cool. Combine shallot mixture, bok choy, seafood and noodles in large bowl, add dressing; mix well.

Dressing: Combine all ingredients in bowl; mix well.

Serves 10.

- Recipe can be made 3 hours ahead.
- Storage: Covered, in refrigerator.
- Freeze: Not suitable.
- Microwave: Not suitable.

BEEF

Main course decisions will be wonderfully easy with our beef recipes. The choice is fresh, interesting and often international, with lots of hot 'n' hearty eating, plus barbecue treats and salads for summer pleasure. Many of the dishes are a meal in themselves, and you won't need to do much more than serve them with a salad, wine and bread rolls.

PEPPER AND BEEF SALAD

4 x 500g pieces of beef eye-fillet
2 tablespoons olive oil
4 medium zucchini
4 baby eggplants
¼ cup (60ml) olive oil, extra
2 medium red peppers, thickly sliced
2 medium yellow peppers,
  thickly sliced
1 lettuce

MARINADE
½ cup fresh oregano leaves
⅓ cup fresh rosemary sprigs
¼ cup fresh tarragon leaves
2 teaspoons black peppercorns
1 tablespoon seeded mustard
2 tablespoons olive oil

RED PEPPER MAYONNAISE
1 medium red pepper
1 cup (250ml) mayonnaise
1 tablespoon tarragon vinegar

Tie beef with string at 3cm intervals. Rub marinade over beef, cover, refrigerate 3 hours.

Heat oil in pan, add beef, cook until browned all over. Transfer beef to wire rack in baking dish, bake, uncovered, in moderately hot oven about 30 minutes or until tender; cool. Cover, refrigerate beef 1 hour.

Slice zucchini and eggplants lengthways. Heat griddle pan, brush with extra oil, add zucchini, eggplants and peppers in batches, cook until tender; cool. (Or, grill or barbecue zucchini, eggplants and peppers, brushing first with oil.)

Just before serving, place lettuce on plate, top with beef and vegetables, drizzle with red pepper mayonnaise.
Marinade: Blend or process all ingredients until smooth.
Red Pepper Mayonnaise: Quarter pepper, remove seeds and membranes. Grill pepper, skin side up, until skin blisters and blackens. Peel away skin. Blend or process pepper, mayonnaise and vinegar until smooth.
Serves 10.
■ Recipe can be made a day ahead.
■ Storage: Covered, separately, in refrigerator.
■ Freeze: Not suitable.
■ Microwave: Not suitable.

RIGHT: Pepper and Beef Salad.

Platter from Home & Garden on the Mall; glassware from Bohemia Crystal Shop.

CHILLI BEEF SLICE

1½ cups (300g) short-grain rice
1 egg
¼ cup (10g) flaked coconut

FILLING
1 tablespoon vegetable oil
1kg minced beef
2 medium onions, chopped
2 cloves garlic, crushed
2 teaspoons ground cumin
2 teaspoons ground coriander
1 teaspoon garam masala
2 teaspoons chilli flakes
2 x 425g cans tomatoes
1 cup (250ml) water
1 egg

TOPPING
125g butter
½ cup (75g) plain flour
1 litre (4 cups) milk
2 eggs
¼ cup chopped fresh coriander

Add rice to pan of boiling water, boil, un-covered, until tender; drain well, do not rinse. Combine warm rice with egg in bowl; mix well. Press rice mixture over base of greased shallow ovenproof dish (3 litre/12 cup capacity). Spread filling over rice, pour over topping, smooth surface, sprinkle with coconut. Bake slice, uncovered, in moderate oven about 1 hour or until lightly browned and set. Stand 10 minutes before serving.

Filling: Heat oil in large pan, add mince in batches, cook, stirring, until well browned. Remove mince from pan with slotted spoon. Add onions, garlic, spices and chilli to same pan, cook, stirring, until onions are soft. Return mince to pan, add un-drained crushed tomatoes and water, simmer, uncovered, until mixture is very thick; cool 5 minutes, stir in egg.

Topping: Melt butter in pan, add flour, cook, stirring, until bubbling. Remove from heat, gradually stir in milk. Stir over heat until mixture boils and thickens; cool 5 minutes, stir in eggs and coriander.

Serves 10.

■ Recipe best made a day ahead.
■ Storage: Covered, in refrigerator.
■ Freeze: Suitable.
■ Microwave: Rice and topping suitable.

RIGHT: Chilli Beef Slice.

Basket and rug from Barbara's Storehouse.

RICH BEEF CASSEROLE WITH BABY VEGETABLES

2.5kg chuck steak
½ cup (125ml) brandy
2½ cups (625ml) dry red wine
2 fresh thyme sprigs
2 bay leaves
1 clove garlic, crushed
2 tablespoons vegetable oil
75g butter, chopped
½ cup (75g) plain flour
1.5 litres (6 cups) beef stock
¼ cup (60ml) tomato paste
12 bacon rashers, chopped
10 (about 250g) small brown onions
400g button mushrooms, quartered
2 bunches (about 400g) baby carrots
20 (about 500g) baby new potatoes
2 tablespoons chopped fresh parsley

Cut steak into 3cm pieces. Combine brandy, wine, thyme, bay leaves and garlic in bowl, add steak, cover; refrigerate 3 hours or overnight.

Drain steak, reserve marinade. Heat oil in large pan, add steak in batches, cook until well browned all over. Transfer steak to ovenproof dish (4.5 litre/18 cup capacity). Melt butter in same pan, add flour, cook, stirring, until dry and grainy. Remove pan from heat, stir in reserved marinade, stir over heat until boiling. Stir in combined stock and paste, pour sauce over steak. Cook, covered, in slow oven 2½ hours.

Add bacon to dry pan, cook until browned and crisp; drain on absorbent paper. Drain all but 2 tablespoons of fat from pan, add onions, cook, stirring, until lightly browned. Add mushrooms, cook, stirring, 2 minutes. Add bacon and onion

mixture to steak mixture, cook, covered, further 30 minutes in slow oven or until meat is tender and sauce thick.

Boil, steam or microwave carrots and potatoes separately until just tender; drain. Serve casserole with carrots and potatoes, sprinkle with parsley.

Serves 10.

- Casserole can be made a day ahead.
- Storage: Covered, in refrigerator.
- Freeze: Suitable.
- Microwave: Carrots and potatoes suitable.

BELOW: Rich Beef Casserole with Baby Vegetables

ORIENTAL BEEF STIR-FRY

2kg rump steak, thinly sliced
¼ cup (60ml) vegetable oil
2 medium carrots
4 large onions, sliced
⅓ cup chopped fresh coriander
10 green shallots, chopped
2 large red peppers, sliced
2 large green peppers, sliced
1 large yellow pepper, sliced
400g snow peas, sliced
4 large tomatoes, sliced
½ cup chopped fresh mint

MARINADE
1 tablespoon grated fresh ginger
4 cloves garlic, crushed
⅓ cup (80ml) lemon juice
3 teaspoons turmeric
2 teaspoons ground coriander
3 teaspoons garam masala
2 teaspoons cracked black pepper
1 teaspoon chilli powder
⅓ cup (80ml) fish sauce

Add steak to marinade in bowl; cover, refrigerate 3 hours or overnight.

Heat 1 tablespoon of the oil in large wok or pan, add one-third undrained steak, stir-fry until steak is browned; remove from pan. Repeat with remaining oil and steak.

Cut carrots into long, thin strips. Add onions and coriander to same pan, cook, stirring, 3 minutes. Add carrots, shallots, peppers and snow peas, cook, stirring, 2 minutes. Return steak to pan, add tomatoes and mint, cook until hot.

Marinade: Combine all ingredients in large bowl.

Serves 10.

- Steak can be marinated a day ahead.
- Storage: Covered, in refrigerator.
- Freeze: Not suitable.
- Microwave: Not suitable.

SATAY BEEF KEBABS WITH PEANUT SAUCE

Soak wooden skewers well in cold water to prevent burning.

2kg rump steak
¼ cup (60ml) olive oil
3 teaspoons seasoned pepper

PEANUT SAUCE
1 cup (150g) unsalted peanuts
½ cup (125ml) peanut butter
2 cups (500ml) chicken stock
2 tablespoons lime juice
2 tablespoons brown sugar
1 large onion, finely chopped
1 clove garlic, crushed
2 teaspoons ground cumin
3 teaspoons curry powder

Cut steak into thin strips, thread onto 50 skewers; brush with combined oil and pepper. Barbecue or grill kebabs until cooked as desired. Serve kebabs with peanut sauce.

Peanut Sauce: Place peanuts on oven tray, bake, uncovered, in hot oven 10 minutes or until peanuts are lightly browned. Blend or process peanuts until finely chopped. Combine peanuts and remaining ingredients in pan, bring to boil, then simmer, uncovered, about 10 minutes or until sauce is thick.

Serves 10.

- Kebabs and sauce can be prepared a day ahead.
- Storage: Covered, separately, in refrigerator.
- Freeze: Not suitable.
- Microwave: Not suitable.

SPICED BARBECUED STEAK

2kg sliced rump steaks
½ cup (125ml) olive oil
½ cup (125ml) lemon juice
1 medium onion, finely chopped
2 cloves garlic, crushed
2 tablespoons dark soy sauce
¼ cup chopped fresh parsley
1 tablespoon chopped fresh oregano
1 tablespoon grated fresh ginger
2 teaspoons ground cumin
½ teaspoon chilli powder
2 teaspoons paprika

Combine all ingredients in shallow dish; cover, refrigerate 4 hours.

Remove steaks from marinade; reserve marinade. Barbecue or grill steaks until cooked as desired. Stand steaks 5 minutes, cut into 1cm slices.

Meanwhile, place reserved marinade in pan, bring to boil, simmer, uncovered, 1 minute. Serve steak with marinade.

Serves 10.

■ Recipe best prepared several hours ahead.
■ Storage: Covered, in refrigerator.
■ Freeze: Uncooked, marinated steak suitable.
■ Microwave: Not suitable.

FAR LEFT: Oriental Beef Stir-Fry.
LEFT: Satay Beef Kebabs with Peanut Sauce.
ABOVE: Spiced Barbecued Steak.

Far left: Glass bowls from Lady Chef; serviettes and basket from Barbara's Storehouse. Left: Pottery and wood from Kenwick Galleries. Above: China from Villeroy & Boch; glasses from Waterford Wedgwood; trivets from Parker's of Turramurra.

OXTAIL CASSEROLE WITH PARSNIP PUREE

4kg oxtail pieces
plain flour
2 tablespoons vegetable oil
1 tablespoon vegetable oil, extra
2 medium onions, sliced
4 cloves garlic, crushed
4 bacon rashers, chopped
2 sticks celery, chopped
2 medium carrots, chopped
2 tablespoons chopped
   fresh rosemary
2 tablespoons chopped fresh thyme
2 tablespoons chopped fresh oregano
2 cups (500ml) dry red wine
1.25 litres (5 cups) beef stock
2 x 410g cans tomatoes
⅓ cup (80ml) tomato paste

PARSNIP PUREE
1 large potato, chopped
1kg (about 5 medium) parsnips,
   chopped
40g butter
¾ cup (180ml) cream
pinch nutmeg

Trim excess fat from oxtail. Toss oxtail in flour, shake away excess flour. Heat oil in pan, add oxtail in batches, cook until browned all over; drain on absorbent paper.

Heat extra oil in pan, add onions, garlic, bacon, celery and carrots, cook until onions are soft. Add herbs, wine, stock, undrained crushed tomatoes, paste and oxtail. Simmer, covered, 1½ hours. Simmer, uncovered, 1 hour or until oxtail is tender and sauce thick; skim away fat. Serve with parsnip puree.

Parsnip Puree: Boil, steam or microwave potato and parsnips until tender; drain. Process potato, parsnips and butter until smooth. Add cream and nutmeg, process until combined.

Serves 10.

- Oxtail casserole can be made 2 days ahead. Parsnip puree can be made a day ahead.
- Storage: Covered, separately, in refrigerator.
- Freeze: Oxtail casserole suitable.
- Microwave: Potato and parsnips suitable.

BEEF FILLET WITH RED ONION RELISH

4 x 500g pieces of beef eye-fillet
2½ teaspoons five-spice powder
1½ teaspoons cracked black pepper
2 tablespoons vegetable oil
1 tablespoon sesame oil
2 tablespoons dark soy sauce
¼ cup (35g) sesame seeds, toasted

RED ONION RELISH
2 teaspoons vegetable oil
2 teaspoons sesame oil
4 medium (about 600g) red Spanish
   onions, sliced
¼ cup (60ml) red wine vinegar
½ cup (125ml) rice wine vinegar
¼ cup (60ml) mirin
¼ teaspoon chilli flakes
½ teaspoon cracked black pepper
2 star anise
¼ cup (55g) sugar

Tie beef with string at 3cm intervals. Sprinkle combined spice powder and pepper all over beef. Heat vegetable oil in pan, add beef, cook, turning, until browned all over. Place beef on wire rack in baking dish, brush with combined sesame oil and sauce. Bake, uncovered, in moderately hot oven about 30 minutes or until cooked as desired. Remove beef from oven, stand, covered, 10 minutes. Sprinkle with seeds, serve warm or cold with red onion relish.

Red Onion Relish: Heat oils in pan, add onions, cook, covered, stirring occasionally, about 15 minutes or until soft. Add remaining ingredients, simmer, uncovered, about 20 minutes or until thick. Discard star anise. Serve warm or cold.

Serves 10.

- Beef can be cooked a day ahead. Relish can be made 3 days ahead.
- Storage: Covered, separately, in refrigerator.
- Freeze: Not suitable.
- Microwave: Not suitable.

LEFT: Oxtail Casserole with Parsnip Puree.
BELOW: Beef Fillet with Red Onion Relish.

Left: China from Villeroy & Boch; glasses from Waterford Wedgwood; serviettes from Between the Sheets.

APRICOT-GLAZED CORNED BEEF

2 x 1.5kg pieces of uncooked
   corned beef
¾ cup (180ml) brown vinegar
⅔ cup (130g) firmly packed
   brown sugar
4 star anise
1 teaspoon black peppercorns
2 cinnamon sticks
1 medium onion, quartered
4 dried red chillies
10cm (about 80g) fresh
   ginger, chopped
¾ cup (180ml) dry white wine
2 tablespoons chopped fresh parsley

APRICOT GLAZE
1 cup (250ml) apricot jam
¼ cup (60ml) French mustard
2 tablespoons brown sugar

Place beef in large pan, add vinegar, sugar, star anise, peppercorns, cinnamon, onion, chillies and ginger, add enough cold water to cover beef. Bring to boil, simmer, covered, about 45 minutes or until beef is just cooked. Cool beef in cooking liquid.

Drain beef, discard cooking liquid. Place beef in shallow baking dish, brush liberally with some of the apricot glaze. Bake, uncovered, in moderate oven about 30 minutes or until beef is heated through;

remove from dish. Add wine and remaining glaze to same dish, stir until heated through; stir in parsley. Serve beef with apricot glaze.

Apricot Glaze: Combine all ingredients in small pan, stir over heat until just hot.

Serves 10.

- Recipe can be made 2 days ahead.
- Storage: Covered, separately, in refrigerator.
- Freeze: Not suitable.
- Microwave: Suitable.

THAI-STYLE RARE BEEF SALAD

You need about 8 limes for this recipe.

2 tablespoons vegetable oil
2kg rump steaks
375g packet fresh egg noodles
2 bunches (about 500g)
    fresh asparagus
3 medium carrots
2 large red peppers, thinly sliced
3 cups (300g) bean sprouts
125g snow peas, sliced
1 bunch (about 15) radishes,
    thinly sliced
1 cup (150g) roasted
    unsalted cashews

DRESSING
3 small fresh red chillies,
    seeded, chopped
1 cup (250ml) lime juice
2/3 cup (130g) firmly packed
    brown sugar
2 tablespoons fish sauce
2 stems fresh lemon grass, chopped

Heat oil in pan, add steaks in batches, cook until browned on both sides and just tender, remove from pan; cool. Cut steaks into thin strips.

Add noodles to pan of boiling water, boil, uncovered, about 5 minutes or until tender; drain, rinse under cold water, drain well. Cut noodles into 15cm lengths with scissors. Boil, steam or microwave asparagus until just tender; drain, rinse under cold water, drain well. Cut carrots into long thin strips.

Combine steak, noodles, asparagus, carrots and remaining ingredients in large bowl, add dressing; mix well.

Dressing: Combine all ingredients in bowl; mix well.

Serves 10.

- Recipe can be made 3 hours ahead.
- Storage: Covered, in refrigerator.
- Freeze: Not suitable.
- Microwave: Noodles and asparagus suitable.

BEEF AND MUSHROOM PIE

4 sheets ready-rolled
    shortcrust pastry
2kg chuck steak
1 tablespoon vegetable oil
3 medium onions
4 cloves garlic, crushed
6 bacon rashers, chopped
2 cups (500ml) beef stock
1/3 cup (80ml) tomato paste
1 tablespoon Worcestershire sauce
2 medium tomatoes, peeled, chopped
400g button mushrooms, halved
1/2 cup (75g) plain flour
1/2 cup (125ml) water
1 egg, lightly beaten
3 sheets ready-rolled puff pastry

Lightly grease 2 x deep 24cm pie dishes. Join 2 sheets of shortcrust pastry together to fit side and base of 1 prepared dish. Repeat with remaining shortcrust pastry and dish. Line pastry with paper, fill with dried beans or rice. Bake in moderately hot oven 10 minutes, remove paper and beans, bake further 10 minutes or until lightly browned; cool.

Cut steak into 2cm pieces. Heat oil in pan, add steak in batches, cook until well browned; remove from pan. Cut onions into wedges. Reheat same pan, add onions, garlic and bacon, cook, stirring, until onions are soft. Return steak to pan, add stock, paste, sauce and tomatoes, simmer, covered, 1½ to 2 hours or until steak is tender. Stir in mushrooms and blended flour and water, stir over high heat until mixture boils and thickens; cool to room temperature.

Divide steak mixture between pastry cases, brush edges with some of the egg. Top with puff pastry; trim edges. Decorate edges with remaining puff pastry. Brush pies with remaining egg, bake in hot oven 10 minutes, reduce to moderately hot, bake further 20 minutes or until pastry is browned and steak mixture heated through.

Serves 10.

- Steak mixture can be made a day ahead.
- Storage: Covered, in refrigerator.
- Freeze: Cooked pies suitable.
- Microwave: Not suitable.

FAR LEFT, TOP: Apricot-Glazed Corned Beef.
FAR LEFT: Thai-Style Rare Beef Salad.
LEFT: Beef and Mushroom Pie.

Far left, top: Platter from Lady Chef; glasses from Bohemia Crystal Shop. Far left: China and glasses from Royal Copenhagen; brass boxes from Parkers of Turramurra; brass candlesticks from The Cottage Manner; serviettes from Between the Sheets.

SPICY SAUSAGE AND SPINACH ROULADE

250g spicy Italian sausages
750g minced beef
1 cup (70g) stale breadcrumbs
2 eggs, lightly beaten
1 tablespoon olive oil

FILLING
250g packet frozen spinach, thawed
2 tablespoons olive oil
1 clove garlic, crushed
150g prosciutto, finely chopped
⅓ cup (50g) pine nuts
½ cup (80g) pitted black olives, chopped
¼ cup (20g) grated parmesan cheese

Squeeze mince mixture out of Italian sausage casings; discard casings. Combine the sausage mince, minced beef, breadcrumbs and eggs in bowl; mix well. Flatten mince mixture on a large sheet of baking paper to 25cm x 35cm rectangle; refrigerate 1 hour.

Sprinkle filling over mince, leaving 1cm border around edge; gently press filling onto mince. Roll mince from a short side, using paper as a guide; pinch edges to seal. Gently place roll on baking tray, seam side down, brush with oil. Bake, uncovered, in moderate oven about 1 hour or until cooked through; cool.

Filling: Drain spinach, add to dry pan; stir over heat until excess liquid is evaporated. Heat oil in separate pan, add garlic and prosciutto, cook, stirring, 2 minutes. Add nuts, cook, stirring, until nuts are lightly browned; cool. Add spinach, olives and cheese; mix well.

Serves 10.
- Recipe can be made 2 days ahead.
- Storage: Covered, in refrigerator.
- Freeze: Suitable.
- Microwave: Not suitable.

RIGHT: Braised Beef with Buttery Mixed Mushrooms.
BELOW: Spicy Sausage and Spinach Roulade.

Right: China and glasses from Waterford Wedgwood; tray from Parker's of Turramurra; serviettes from Between the Sheets. Below: Platter and serviette from Barbara's Storehouse; glasses from Bohemia Crystal Shop.

BRAISED BEEF WITH BUTTERY MIXED MUSHROOMS

8 fresh thyme sprigs
3 fresh oregano sprigs
2 bay leaves
⅓ cup (80ml) vegetable oil
2 medium onions, sliced
3 cloves garlic, sliced
2kg piece of rolled beef topside
1 cup (250ml) dry red wine
2¼ cups (560ml) beef stock
⅓ cup (80ml) dry red wine, extra
2½ tablespoons cornflour
¼ cup (60ml) water

BUTTERY MIXED MUSHROOMS
100g butter
150g oyster mushrooms, halved
200g Swiss brown mushrooms, quartered
100g shitake mushrooms, sliced
350g button mushrooms, halved
2 tablespoons chopped fresh parsley
2 tablespoons chopped fresh thyme

Tie herbs together with string. Heat half the oil in pan, add onions and garlic, cook, stirring, until onions are soft; drain on absorbent paper. Heat remaining oil in pan, add beef, cook, turning, until browned all over. Return onion mixture to pan, add herbs, wine and stock, cook, covered, over low heat, turning beef once, about 2 hours or until beef is tender. Discard herbs from pan. Remove beef. Strain sauce, pushing solids through strainer, into small pan (you will need 1 litre/4 cups of sauce). Add extra wine to pan, bring to boil, stir in blended cornflour and water, stir over heat until sauce boils and thickens. Serve beef with sauce and mushrooms.

Buttery Mixed Mushrooms: Heat butter in pan, add mushrooms, cook, stirring, until tender; stir in herbs.

Serves 10.

▨ Mushrooms can be cooked a day ahead; reheat before serving.
▨ Storage: Covered, in refrigerator.
▨ Freeze: Not suitable.
▨ Microwave: Mushrooms suitable.

LAMB

A tender, flavourful lamb dish is always popular and, here again, we have included ideas that give you a terrific main course with just one recipe. Some are casual; others, more elegant, are ideal for a sit-down dinner. Large cuts such as a shoulder, loin or leg are easier to cut and serve if they are boned or butterflied as we specify, and you can ask your butcher to do this for you.

POPPY SEED BLINIS WITH LAMB SALAD

2 tablespoons vegetable oil
1.25kg lamb fillets
1 bunch (about 15) radishes
200g snow pea sprouts
200g alfalfa sprouts
¼ cup chopped fresh basil
2 tablespoons chopped fresh parsley
¼ cup (35g) sesame seeds, toasted

DRESSING
1 cup (250ml) olive oil
½ cup (125ml) cider vinegar
2 teaspoons sugar
1 teaspoon sesame oil

BLINIS
1 tablespoon (14g) dried yeast
1 teaspoon sugar
1⅔ cups (410ml) warm milk
2 eggs, separated
2 egg yolks
300ml sour cream
2 cups (300g) plain flour
1 teaspoon salt
⅓ cup (50g) poppy seeds

Heat oil in pan, add lamb in batches, cook until browned all over and tender. Cool lamb, slice thinly.

Slice radishes thinly, cut slices into thin strips. Combine lamb, radishes, sprouts, herbs and seeds in bowl, add half the dressing; mix well.

Place 2 blinis on each serving plate, top evenly with lamb mixture; drizzle with remaining dressing.

Dressing: Combine all ingredients in jar; shake well.
Blinis: Combine yeast, sugar and milk in bowl, cover, stand in warm place about 10 minutes or until mixture is frothy. Combine the 4 egg yolks with sour cream, stir into yeast mixture.

Sift flour and salt into large bowl, add poppy seeds. Gradually stir in sour cream mixture; mix until smooth. Cover, stand in warm place about 1 hour or until batter is risen and bubbly.

Beat egg whites in small bowl with electric mixer until soft peaks form, fold into batter. Drop ¼ cup (60ml) of batter into heated greased heavy-based pan, cook until lightly browned underneath, turn blini, brown other side. Repeat with remaining batter. You need 20 blinis for this recipe.

Serves 10.

- Dressing can be made 2 days ahead. Lamb can be cooked a day ahead. Blinis best made on day of serving.
- Storage: Covered, separately, in refrigerator.
- Freeze: Blinis suitable.
- Microwave: Not suitable.

RIGHT: Poppy Seed Blinis with Lamb Salad.

Plates by Ventura Design; tiles from Pazotti; serviettes, flower tub and servers from Accoutrement.

BRAISED MUSTARD LAMB WITH CELERIAC

2 tablespoons vegetable oil
1 medium onion, sliced
3 cloves garlic, crushed
2 x 1kg boned rolled shoulders
of lamb
1 cup (250ml) dry white wine
1½ tablespoons chopped
fresh rosemary
1½ tablespoons chopped
fresh thyme
1 teaspoon celery seeds
2½ cups (625ml) beef stock
½ cup (125ml) water
4 medium celeriac, sliced
½ cup (125ml) cream
1 tablespoon cornflour
2 tablespoons water, extra
¼ cup (60ml) seeded mustard
2 tablespoons chopped fresh parsley

BRAISED ONIONS
2 tablespoons olive oil
1kg baby onions
½ cup (125ml) dry white wine
½ cup (125ml) beef stock

Heat oil in large pan, add onion and garlic, cook, stirring, until onion is soft; drain on absorbent paper. Add lamb to same pan, cook, turning, until browned all over. Return onion mixture to pan, add wine, herbs, seeds, stock and water, simmer, covered, 1 hour.

Add celeriac, simmer, covered, further 20 minutes or until lamb and celeriac are tender. Remove lamb and celeriac from pan using slotted spoon; keep warm.

Strain cooking liquid into small pan (you will need 3½ cups/875ml), add cream, simmer, uncovered, 5 minutes. Stir in blended cornflour and extra water, stir over heat until sauce boils and thickens, stir in mustard. Serve lamb sliced with celeriac, sauce and braised onions, sprinkle with parsley.

Braised Onions: Heat oil in pan, add onions, cook, stirring, about 10 minutes or until browned. Add wine and stock, simmer, covered, 30 minutes. Simmer, uncovered, further 10 minutes or until almost all liquid is evaporated.

Serves 10.

- ■ Recipe can be prepared a day ahead. Celeriac best added on day of serving.
- ■ Storage: Covered, in refrigerator.
- ■ Freeze: Not suitable.
- ■ Microwave: Not suitable.

BELOW: Braised Mustard Lamb with Celeriac.
RIGHT: Barbecued Lamb with Coriander Pesto.

Below: Plates, tablecloth and serviettes from Accoutrement; serviette rings from Home & Garden on the Mall. Right: Plates from Ventura Design.

BARBECUED LAMB WITH CORIANDER PESTO

2 x 2kg legs of lamb, butterflied
salt, pepper

CORIANDER PESTO
2 cups firmly packed fresh
coriander leaves
1 cup firmly packed fresh
parsley sprigs
1 cup (155g) pine nuts, toasted
2 cloves garlic, crushed
1 cup (250ml) olive oil
¼ cup (60ml) lemon juice
1 teaspoon sugar

Cover lamb with plastic wrap. Using a meat mallet, pound lamb to uniform thickness. Cut each leg in half crossways, season with salt and pepper, barbecue until cooked as desired. Serve with coriander pesto.

Coriander Pesto: Blend or process herbs, nuts and garlic until finely chopped. Gradually add oil in a thin stream while motor is operating, blend until combined. Add juice and sugar, blend until smooth.

Serves 10.

- ■ Pesto can be made 2 days ahead.
- ■ Storage: Covered, in refrigerator.
- ■ Freeze: Pesto suitable.
- ■ Microwave: Not suitable.

LAMB PARCELS WITH MINT JELLY

250g cauliflower, chopped
2 tablespoons vegetable oil
4 cloves garlic, crushed
1 medium leek, sliced
750g minced lamb
2 medium carrots, grated
2 medium zucchini, grated
1 cup (70g) stale breadcrumbs
2 tablespoons chopped
** fresh rosemary**
1 tablespoon chopped fresh thyme
24 sheets fillo pastry
125g butter, melted

MINT JELLY
1kg apples
1.5 litres (6 cups) water
½ cup (125ml) lemon juice
⅔ cup chopped fresh mint
3 cups (660g) sugar, approximately
2 tablespoons chopped fresh
** mint, extra**

Boil, steam or microwave cauliflower until just tender; drain. Heat oil in pan, add garlic and leek, cook, stirring, until leek is soft. Add lamb, cook, stirring, until well browned, stir in carrots and zucchini, cook, stirring, 3 minutes. Stir in cauliflower, breadcrumbs and herbs; cool.

Layer 2 pastry sheets together, brushing each with butter. Fold layered pastry in half crossways, brush with more butter. Place ½ cup (125ml) of lamb mixture at 1 end of pastry. Fold end over to form a triangle, continue folding until end of pastry, brush with more butter; place on greased oven tray. Repeat with remaining pastry sheets, butter and filling. Bake, uncovered, in moderately hot oven about 20 minutes or until lightly browned and crisp. Serve with mint jelly.

Mint Jelly: Chop unpeeled apples, do not discard seeds. Combine apples, seeds, water, juice and mint in large pan, simmer, covered, about 40 minutes or until apples are very soft. Strain mixture through a fine cloth into large bowl. Allow liquid to drip through cloth slowly; do not squeeze pulp.

Measure liquid, pour into large pan. Add ¾ cup (165g) sugar to each 1 cup (250ml) liquid. Stir over low heat, without boiling, until sugar is dissolved, then boil, uncovered, without stirring, about 30 minutes or until jelly sets when tested on a cold saucer. Remove from heat, stand 10 minutes. Stir in extra mint. Pour into hot sterilised jars; seal while hot.

Makes about 3½ cups (875ml).

Makes 12.

- Lamb parcels can be prepared a day ahead. Mint jelly can be made 2 weeks ahead.
- Storage: Covered, separately, in refrigerator.
- Freeze: Uncooked lamb parcels suitable.
- Microwave: Cauliflower suitable.

CHILLI LAMB WITH SESAME VEGETABLES

3 (about 2kg) loins of lamb, boned

MARINADE
2 tablespoons grated fresh ginger
4 cloves garlic, crushed
½ cup (125ml) teriyaki sauce
¼ cup (60ml) mild sweet chilli sauce
¼ cup (60ml) honey
1 teaspoon sesame oil
2 tablespoons oyster sauce

SESAME VEGETABLES
3 medium carrots
3 medium zucchini
4 sticks celery
1 tablespoon vegetable oil
1 tablespoon light soy sauce
2 tablespoons sesame seeds, toasted

Roll up lamb, secure with string at 3cm intervals. Place lamb in shallow ovenproof dish, pour over marinade; cover, refrigerate several hours or overnight.

Bake undrained lamb in moderately hot oven about 45 minutes or until tender; stand 10 minutes. Serve sliced, drizzled with ½ cup (125ml) of the pan juices. Serve with sesame vegetables.

Marinade: Combine all ingredients in bowl; mix well.

Sesame Vegetables: Cut vegetables into 5mm strips. Heat oil in pan, add carrots, cook, stirring, 2 minutes. Add zucchini and celery, cook, stirring, until vegetables are just tender, stir in sauce and seeds.

Serves 10.

■ Recipe can be prepared a day ahead.
■ Storage: Covered, in refrigerator.
■ Freeze: Not suitable.
■ Microwave: Vegetables suitable.

LEFT: Lamb Parcels with Mint Jelly.
BELOW: Chilli Lamb with Sesame Vegetables.

Left: China from Corso de Fiori; rack from Le Forge. Below: Platter, bottle and servers from Accoutrement; jug, glasses, rug and wooden mat from Home & Garden on the Mall; plates from Country Floors.

BARBECUED LAMB WITH BUTTER BEANS

½ cup (125ml) olive oil
¼ cup (60ml) tomato sauce
2 tablespoons lemon juice
2 cloves garlic, crushed
1 teaspoon dried oregano leaves
½ teaspoon paprika
1.5kg lamb fillets

BUTTER BEANS
4 medium leeks, sliced
2 cloves garlic, crushed
2 cups (500ml) chicken stock
1 teaspoon paprika
500g button mushrooms, quartered
8 medium tomatoes, peeled, chopped
4 x 310g cans butter beans,
    rinsed, drained
¼ cup chopped fresh parsley

Combine oil, sauce, juice, garlic, oregano and paprika in large bowl. Add lamb, mix well. Cover, refrigerate 3 hours or overnight.

Remove lamb from marinade, discard marinade. Barbecue or grill lamb until cooked. Serve lamb with butter beans.

Butter Beans: Combine leeks, garlic, stock and paprika in pan, simmer, uncovered, stirring occasionally, until leeks are tender and almost all the liquid is evaporated. Add mushrooms, cook, stirring, until tender. Add tomatoes and beans, simmer, uncovered, until mixture is slightly thickened; stir in parsley.

TANDOORI LAMB KEBABS WITH CHICK PEA SALAD

3kg lamb leg steaks
1 cup (250ml) tandoori paste
2 cups (500ml) plain yogurt
4 medium onions
20 pitta pocket breads

RAITA
2 medium cucumbers, peeled,
    seeded, chopped
coarse cooking salt
1 medium apple, peeled, grated
1 tablespoon lemon juice
2 cups (500ml) plain yogurt
¼ cup chopped fresh mint

CHICK PEA SALAD
⅔ cup (160ml) light olive oil
2 medium onions, finely chopped
2 cloves garlic, crushed
1 tablespoon ground coriander
2 teaspoons cumin seeds, toasted
2 teaspoons paprika
2 teaspoons ground ginger
1 teaspoon garam masala
1 teaspoon turmeric
1 teaspoon sugar
pinch cayenne pepper
1 tablespoon lemon juice
3 medium tomatoes,
    seeded, chopped
⅓ cup chopped fresh parsley
4 x 310g cans chick peas,
    rinsed, drained

Cut lamb into 2cm pieces. Combine lamb, paste and yogurt in large bowl; mix well. Cover, refrigerate 3 hours or overnight.

Remove lamb from marinade, discard marinade. Cut onions into wedges. Thread lamb and onions onto 20 skewers.

Just before serving, grill or barbecue kebabs until cooked as desired. Serve with pitta pocket breads, raita and chick pea salad.

Raita: Sprinkle cucumbers with salt, stand 1 hour. Rinse cucumbers under cold water; drain, pat dry with absorbent paper. Combine cucumbers and remaining ingredients in bowl; mix well.

Chick Pea Salad: Heat 2 tablespoons of the oil in pan, add onions and garlic, cook, stirring, until onions are soft. Combine onion mixture, remaining oil, spices, sugar, pepper and juice in bowl; mix well. Add tomatoes, parsley and chick peas; mix to combine.

Serves 10.

■ Recipe can be prepared a day ahead.
■ Storage: Covered, separately,
    in refrigerator.
■ Freeze: Not suitable.
■ Microwave: Not suitable.

Serves 10.

- Lamb and butter beans can be prepared a day ahead.
- Storage: Covered, separately, in refrigerator.
- Freeze: Uncooked, marinated lamb suitable.
- Microwave: Not suitable.

LEFT: Tandoori Lamb Kebabs with Chick Pea Salad.
RIGHT: Barbecued Lamb with Butter Beans.
BELOW: Lamb Sausage and Bean Bake.

Left: Plates from Ventura Design. Right: Serviettes from Home & Garden on the Mall. Below: Plates from Corso de Fiori.

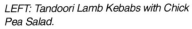

LAMB SAUSAGE AND BEAN BAKE

3 medium red peppers
1 tablespoon vegetable oil
1.6kg lamb sausages
2 medium onions, sliced
200g chorizo sausages, chopped
3 teaspoons ground cumin
3 teaspoons paprika
1/2 teaspoon chilli powder
3 x 410g cans tomatoes
1 1/2 cups (375ml) beef stock
2 x 310g cans red kidney beans, rinsed, drained
1/2 cup chopped fresh coriander

CORN CHIP TOPPING
1 1/2 cups (185g) grated tasty cheddar cheese
200g packet corn chips, crushed
1/3 cup chopped fresh parsley
2 tablespoons chopped fresh basil

Quarter peppers, remove seeds and membranes. Grill peppers, skin side up, until skin blisters and blackens. Peel away skin, slice peppers.

Heat oil in pan, add sausages in batches, cook until browned all over and almost cooked through. Drain on absorbent paper; slice sausages.

Drain all but 1 tablespoon of oil from pan, add onions and chorizo, cook, stirring, until onions are soft. Add spices, cook, stirring, until fragrant. Add peppers, undrained crushed tomatoes and stock, simmer, uncovered, about 10 minutes or until slightly thickened. Stir in sausages, beans and coriander. Spoon mixture into ovenproof dish (4 litre/16 cup capacity).

Just before serving, sprinkle with corn chip topping, bake, uncovered, in moderate oven about 30 minutes or until lightly browned and heated through.
Corn Chip Topping: Combine all ingredients in bowl; mix well.

Serves 10.

- Recipe, without topping, can be prepared 2 days ahead.
- Storage: Covered, in refrigerator.
- Freeze: Not suitable.
- Microwave: Not suitable.

LAMB CUTLETS WITH COUSCOUS TABBOULEH

30 lamb cutlets
1¼ cups (310ml) light olive oil
½ cup (125ml) lemon juice
2 teaspoons chicken stock powder
4 cloves garlic, crushed
2 tablespoons chopped
fresh coriander
2 tablespoons chopped fresh basil

YOGURT SAUCE
⅓ cup (80ml) tahini paste
2 tablespoons lemon juice
1 cup (250ml) plain yogurt
2 cloves garlic, crushed
2 tablespoons chopped
fresh coriander

COUSCOUS TABBOULEH
1½ cups (275g) couscous
1 cup (250ml) boiling water
8 green shallots, chopped
2 medium tomatoes,
seeded, chopped
1 medium yellow pepper, chopped
½ cup (125ml) olive oil
¼ cup (60ml) lemon juice
2 cups chopped fresh
flat-leafed parsley
¼ cup chopped fresh mint

Place cutlets in single layer in shallow dish. Pour combined remaining ingredients over cutlets; cover, refrigerate several hours or overnight.

Drain cutlets, discard marinade. Grill or barbecue cutlets until cooked as desired. Serve hot or cold with yogurt sauce and couscous tabbouleh.

Yogurt Sauce: Combine all ingredients in small bowl; mix well.

Couscous Tabbouleh: Combine couscous and water in heatproof bowl, stand 10 minutes. Combine couscous mixture and remaining ingredients in large bowl; mix well.

Serves 10.

- Recipe can be made a day ahead.
- Storage: Covered, separately, in refrigerator.
- Freeze: Not suitable.
- Microwave: Not suitable.

70

MONGOLIAN LAMB CASEROLE

2 x 2kg legs of lamb, boned
2 tablespoons vegetable oil
1 tablespoon brown sugar
⅓ cup (80ml) light soy sauce
¼ cup (60ml) black bean paste
6 cloves garlic, crushed
8 medium onions, quartered
1½ cups (375ml) chicken stock
½ teaspoon five spice powder
2 tablespoons cornflour
2 tablespoons water
4 green shallots, sliced

Cut lamb into 1cm slices, about 7cm in length. Heat oil in pan, cook lamb in batches until well browned. Return all lamb to pan, add sugar, sauce, paste, garlic, onions, stock and five spice powder, simmer, covered, about 50 minutes or until lamb is tender. Add blended cornflour and water, stir over heat until mixture boils and thickens slightly; serve sprinkled with shallots. Serve with couscous or rice.

Serves 10.

■ Casserole can be made a day ahead.
■ Storage: Covered, in refrigerator.
■ Freeze: Suitable.
■ Microwave: Not suitable.

LEFT: Lamb Cutlets with Couscous Tabbouleh.
BELOW: Mongolian Lamb Casserole.

Left: Rug, basket, glasses and candle holder from Home & Garden on the Mall; tiles from Country Floors; silver spoon from Accoutrement. Below: China and glassware from Corso de Fiori; racks from Le Forge.

PORK & VEAL

Our splendid, orange-glazed ham could easily take pride of place on your table, or perhaps tasty marinated pork ribs would suit the occasion; both are so different. But your choice is wide and wonderful, with robust pork and veal dishes including roasts with unusual accompaniments, generous salads, casseroles and Oriental roast pork accompanied by a particularly delicious fried rice. Again, many dishes are a meal in themselves.

ORANGE-GLAZED BAKED HAM

1 (about 8kg) cooked ham
3 medium oranges, segmented
4 pitted prunes, halved

GLAZE
½ cup (100g) firmly packed brown sugar
⅓ cup (80ml) orange marmalade
⅓ cup (80ml) whisky

To remove rind from ham, run thumb around edge of rind just under skin. Start pulling rind from widest end of ham, using fingers to loosen it from the fat. When you have pulled it to within 15cm of shank end, take a very sharp, pointed knife and cut through rind around shank end of leg in decorative pattern. Continue to pull the rind slowly and carefully away from the fat up to the decorative pattern.

Cut across fat at about 3cm intervals; cut just through the surface of the top fat, not deeply, or the fat will spread apart during cooking.

Place ham on wire rack in large baking dish, brush well with some of the glaze. Bake, uncovered, in moderate oven 50 minutes, brush frequently with glaze. Place orange segments and prunes in decorative pattern over ham; secure with toothpicks. Bake further 15 minutes or until ham is browned. Serve warm or cold.
Glaze: Combine all ingredients in pan, stir over heat, without boiling, until sugar is dissolved. Pour mixture through coarse sieve; cool to room temperature.

Serves 20 to 30.

■ Recipe can be made a day ahead.
■ Storage: Covered, in refrigerator.
■ Freeze: Not suitable.
■ Microwave: Glaze suitable.

RIGHT: Orange-Glazed Baked Ham.

Platter, basket and glasses from The Melbourne Shop.

SPICY PORK AND VEGETABLE CASSEROLE WITH COUSCOUS

1 tablespoon vegetable oil
10 thick pork sausages
¼ cup (60ml) vegetable oil, extra
2 medium onions, sliced
2 teaspoons cumin seeds
1 teaspoon garam masala
1 teaspoon ground coriander
1 medium eggplant, chopped
2 large carrots, chopped
2 medium potatoes, chopped
300g pumpkin, chopped
**2 x 310g cans chick peas,
   rinsed, drained**
2 x 425g cans tomatoes
⅓ cup (80ml) tomato paste
1 teaspoon sambal oelek
100g green beans, chopped
2 medium zucchini, chopped

COUSCOUS
1.25 litres (5 cups) water
1kg couscous
125g butter, chopped
¾ cup chopped fresh parsley

Heat oil in pan, add sausages in batches, cook until browned and cooked through; drain on absorbent paper. Cut sausages into thick slices. Heat extra oil in large pan, add onions and spices, cook, stirring, until onions are soft.

Add eggplant, carrots, potatoes and pumpkin, stir until coated with oil. Cook, covered, over low heat 10 minutes, stirring occasionally. Add chick peas, undrained crushed tomatoes, paste and sambal oelek. Simmer, covered, 20 minutes or until vegetables are just tender.

Add sausages, beans and zucchini, simmer, uncovered, about 10 minutes, stirring occasionally, or until vegetables are tender and sauce slightly thickened. Serve with couscous.

Couscous: Bring the water to boil in pan, remove from heat, stir in couscous and butter, stir about 2 minutes or until grains are tender. Stir in parsley.

Serves 10.

■ Casserole can be made a day ahead.
■ Storage: Covered, in refrigerator.
■ Freeze: Not suitable.
■ Microwave: Not suitable.

ABOVE: Spicy Pork and Vegetable Casserole with Couscous.
RIGHT: Roast Veal with Mustard Fruits.

Above: Plates and basket from The Melbourne Shop. Right: China and glassware from Corso de Fiori; candle holder from Le Forge.

ROAST VEAL WITH MUSTARD FRUITS

3 cloves garlic, crushed
2 tablespoons chopped
    fresh rosemary
2 tablespoons chopped fresh thyme
2 tablespoons chopped fresh sage
2 tablespoons olive oil
2 tablespoons Dijon mustard
2kg boned rolled leg of veal

MUSTARD FRUITS
2 cups (500ml) red wine vinegar
1 cup (250ml) dry red wine
1 cup (250ml) water
2 cups (440g) sugar
2 cinnamon sticks
12 cloves

1 teaspoon black mustard seeds
1 teaspoon cracked black pepper
1 tablespoon grated orange rind
2 teaspoons grated lemon rind
1½ tablespoons dry mustard
2 medium oranges, peeled, sliced
1 large apple, peeled, sliced
2 small pears, peeled, sliced
250g black grapes
250g white grapes

Combine garlic, herbs, oil and mustard in bowl; mix well. Rub garlic mixture all over veal, place veal on wire rack in baking dish, bake, uncovered, in moderate oven about 1½ hours or until cooked as desired. Serve veal warm or cold with mustard fruits.

Mustard Fruits: Combine vinegar, wine, water, sugar, spices, mustard seeds, pepper and rinds in pan, simmer, uncovered, 10 minutes, stir in dry mustard. Pack fruit into large, hot, sterilised jar, cover completely with hot vinegar mixture; seal jar while hot.

Serves 10.

■ Roast veal can be cooked a day ahead. Mustard fruits best made a month ahead.
■ Storage: Veal, covered, in refrigerator. Mustard fruits, dark, cool place; refrigerate after opening.
■ Freeze: Not suitable.
■ Microwave: Not suitable.

POTATO AND EGG SALAD WITH ANCHOVY DRESSING

2 cups (150g) stale breadcrumbs
1 clove garlic, crushed
40g butter, melted
1.5kg green beans
1.5kg baby new potatoes, halved
750g mild salami, chopped
¾ cup chopped fresh
**   flat-leafed parsley**
10 hard-boiled eggs, quartered

ANCHOVY DRESSING
2 eggs
2 cloves garlic, crushed
2 tablespoons lemon juice
1 teaspoon seeded mustard
56g can anchovy fillets, drained
1½ cups (375ml) olive oil
2 tablespoons milk, approximately

Combine breadcrumbs, garlic and butter in bowl; mix well. Heat pan, add breadcrumb mixture, cook, stirring, until lightly browned and crisp. Cut beans into 5cm lengths. Boil, steam or microwave beans and potatoes separately until just tender. Drain vegetables, rinse under cold water, drain. Combine beans, potatoes, salami and parsley in large bowl.

Just before serving, add eggs, drizzle with anchovy dressing; mix gently, sprinkle with breadcrumb mixture.

Anchovy Dressing: Blend or process eggs, garlic, juice, mustard and anchovies until smooth, gradually add oil in a thin stream while motor is operating; blend until smooth. Stir in enough milk to give pouring consistency.

Serves 10.

- Vegetables can be prepared a day ahead. Anchovy dressing can be made 2 days ahead.
- Storage: Covered, separately, in refrigerator.
- Freeze: Not suitable.
- Microwave: Vegetables suitable.

LINGUINE WITH PROSCIUTTO, PEAS AND CREAM

2 tablespoons olive oil
2 medium onions, chopped
3 cloves garlic, crushed
250g sliced prosciutto, chopped
800g button mushrooms, sliced
2 cups (220g) drained sliced
　　sun-dried tomatoes
2 tablespoons chopped fresh thyme
½ cup (125ml) dry white wine
900ml cream
2 cups (250g) frozen green
　　peas, thawed
½ cup shredded fresh basil
1kg linguine pasta
2 cups (160g) grated
　　parmesan cheese

Heat oil in pan, add onions and garlic, cook, stirring, until onions are soft. Add prosciutto and mushrooms, cook, stirring, until mushrooms are soft. Add tomatoes, thyme, wine and cream, simmer, uncovered, 5 minutes, stir in peas and basil, stir until heated through.

Add pasta to large pan of boiling water, boil, uncovered, until just tender; drain. Toss half the cheese and half the mushroom mixture through pasta, top with remaining mushroom mixture and remaining cheese.

Serves 10.

■ Recipe best made just before serving.
■ Freeze: Not suitable.
■ Microwave: Suitable.

LEFT: Potato and Egg Salad with Anchovy Dressing.
ABOVE: Linguine with Prosciutto, Peas and Cream.

Left: China and basket from Freedom Furniture Stores.

MARINATED VEAL AND RATATOUILLE SALAD

2.5kg veal fillets
4 strips orange rind
2 tablespoons orange juice
1 tablespoon cracked black pepper
2 bay leaves
⅓ cup fresh rosemary leaves
1 tablespoon chopped fresh sage
1½ cups (375ml) light olive oil

RATATOUILLE SALAD
2 medium red peppers
2 medium yellow peppers
1 medium green pepper
⅓ cup (80ml) light olive oil
2 medium onions, chopped
10 baby eggplants, sliced
15 small zucchini, sliced
500g cherry tomatoes, halved

PESTO DRESSING
2 cups firmly packed fresh
  basil leaves
½ cup (40g) grated parmesan cheese
½ cup (75g) pine nuts, toasted
2 cloves garlic
1 cup (250ml) olive oil

Place veal in shallow dish, pour over combined remaining ingredients, cover, refrigerate 3 hours or overnight.

Remove veal from marinade; discard marinade. Add veal to hot pan in batches, cook over high heat until browned all over. Transfer veal to baking dish, bake, uncovered, in moderate oven about 10 minutes or until cooked as desired; cool. Cut veal into 1cm slices. Combine veal, ratatouille salad and pesto dressing in bowl; mix gently.

Ratatouille Salad: Quarter peppers, remove seeds and membranes. Grill peppers, skin side up, until skin blisters and blackens. Peel away skin, cut peppers into 2cm squares.

Heat half the oil in pan, add onions and eggplants, cook, stirring, until onions are soft, remove from pan. Heat remaining oil in pan, add zucchini, cook, stirring, until just tender. Combine peppers, onion mixture and zucchini in bowl; cool. Stir in tomatoes.

Pesto Dressing: Blend or process basil, cheese, nuts and garlic until smooth, gradually add oil in a thin stream while motor is operating; blend until combined.

Serves 10.

■ Recipe can be made a day ahead.
■ Storage: Covered, in refrigerator.
■ Freeze: Pesto suitable.
■ Microwave: Not suitable.

ORIENTAL ROAST PORK WITH FRIED RICE

2kg loin of pork, boned, skinned
⅓ cup (80ml) light soy sauce
¼ cup (60ml) sweet sherry
2 tablespoons hoi sin sauce
1 tablespoon grated fresh ginger
4 cloves garlic, crushed
2 teaspoons sesame oil
⅓ cup (80ml) honey
1 teaspoon five spice powder
2 tablespoons teriyaki sauce

FRIED RICE
3 cups (600g) long-grain rice
1.25 litres (5 cups) water
30g Chinese dried mushrooms
1 tablespoon vegetable oil
5 eggs, lightly beaten
2 tablespoons vegetable oil, extra
2 teaspoons sesame oil
2 cloves garlic, crushed
2 tablespoons grated fresh ginger
4 green shallots, chopped
1 large red pepper, chopped
425g can baby corn, drained, chopped
200g snow peas, sliced
⅓ cup (80ml) light soy sauce

Trim fat from pork. Roll pork from long side, tie with string at 3cm intervals. Place pork in large shallow dish, pour over combined remaining ingredients, cover, refrigerate pork several hours or overnight.

Remove pork from marinade, reserve marinade. Place pork on wire rack in baking dish. Bake, uncovered, in moderate oven about 1½ hours or until cooked through; brush occasionally with reserved marinade. Serve with fried rice.

Fried Rice: Wash and rinse rice. Place rice and the 5 cups of water in large pan, bring to boil, simmer, covered, over low heat about 10 minutes or until most of the liquid is absorbed. Remove from heat, stand, covered, 15 minutes. Spread rice

evenly over 2 shallow trays, cover, refrigerate overnight. Stir occasionally to allow rice to dry completely.

Place mushrooms in heatproof bowl, cover with boiling water, stand 20 minutes. Drain mushrooms, remove stems, chop caps.

Heat oil in pan, add eggs, cook, stirring, until creamy, remove from pan. Heat extra oil and sesame oil in large pan, add mushrooms, garlic, ginger, shallots, pepper, corn and snow peas, cook, stirring, 3 minutes. Add rice and sauce, cook, stirring, until vegetables are just tender and rice heated through, stir in eggs.

Serves 10.

- ■ Pork best prepared a day ahead. Rice can be made 2 days ahead.
- ■ Storage: Covered, separately, in refrigerator.
- ■ Freeze: Not suitable
- ■ Microwave: Rice and eggs suitable.

LEFT: Marinated Veal and Ratatouille Salad.
BELOW: Oriental Roast Pork with Fried Rice.

Left: Platter, plates and serving ware from Accoutrement; steel basket from Freedom Furniture Stores. Below: Platter from Accoutrement.

CHUNKY PORK RIBS IN SHERRY GARLIC MARINADE

2kg American-style pork spare ribs
½ cup (125ml) olive oil
⅓ cup (80ml) tomato sauce
¼ cup (60ml) Worcestershire sauce
¼ cup (60ml) dry sherry
1 medium onion, finely chopped
3 cloves garlic, crushed
2 tablespoons brown sugar
2 teaspoons dried oregano leaves
1 teaspoon seasoned pepper

Cut ribs into 2 pieces. Combine ribs with remaining ingredients in bowl; mix well. Cover, refrigerate ribs several hours or overnight.

Remove ribs from marinade, discard marinade. Place ribs on wire rack in baking dish, bake, uncovered, in moderate oven about 50 minutes or until well browned and cooked through.

Serves 10.

- Recipe can be prepared a day ahead.
- Storage: Covered, in refrigerator.
- Freeze: Uncooked, marinated ribs suitable.
- Microwave: Not suitable.

ITALIAN-STYLE PORK STEAKS WITH PROSCIUTTO

1 tablespoon olive oil
10 pork leg steaks
10 slices (about 300g) prosciutto
1 cup (100g) grated
   mozzarella cheese
1 cup (80g) grated parmesan cheese
1 cup (70g) stale breadcrumbs

TOMATO SAUCE
1 tablespoon olive oil
1 medium onion, chopped
2 cloves garlic, crushed
2 x 425g cans tomatoes
1/4 cup (60ml) dry red wine
2 teaspoons sugar
1 tablespoon chopped fresh oregano

Heat oil in pan, add pork in batches, cook until well browned on both sides and tender. Place pork on oven trays, top evenly with tomato sauce, prosciutto and combined cheeses and breadcrumbs.

Just before serving, bake, uncovered, in very hot oven about 5 minutes or until lightly browned and heated through.

Tomato Sauce: Heat oil in pan, add onion and garlic, cook, stirring, until onion is soft. Stir in undrained crushed tomatoes, wine, sugar and oregano, simmer, uncovered, until reduced to 2 1/2 cups (625ml).

Serves 10.

■ Tomato sauce can be made a day ahead. Pork can be prepared several hours ahead.
■ Storage: Covered, separately, in refrigerator.
■ Freeze: Tomato sauce suitable.
■ Microwave: Not suitable.

PORK AND NOODLE SALAD

You need about 4 limes for this recipe.

40g Chinese dried mushrooms
3 cloves garlic
4cm piece (about 30g) fresh ginger
2 tablespoons vegetable oil
2 medium onions, chopped
750g minced pork and veal
1/4 cup (60ml) water
300g cellophane noodles
3 sticks celery, thinly sliced
1/2 cup fresh coriander leaves
10 green shallots, sliced

DRESSING
1/2 cup (125ml) lime juice
1/3 cup (80ml) fish sauce
3 teaspoons palm sugar
1/2 teaspoon chilli powder

Place mushrooms in heatproof bowl, cover with boiling water, stand 20 minutes. Drain mushrooms, discard stems, cut caps into thin strips. Cut garlic and ginger into thin strips. Heat oil in pan, add garlic, ginger, onions, mince and water, cook, stirring, until mince is changed in colour and cooked; drain.

Place noodles in large bowl, cover with boiling water, stand about 3 minutes or until tender; drain well. Cut noodles into 10cm lengths, using scissors.

Combine mince mixture, mushrooms, celery, coriander and shallots in large bowl, stir in dressing; mix well.

Just before serving, stir in noodles. Serve warm or cold.

Dressing: Combine all ingredients in jar; shake well.

Serves 10.

■ Recipe can be prepared 3 hours ahead.
■ Storage: Covered, in refrigerator.
■ Freeze: Not suitable.
■ Microwave: Not suitable.

LEFT: Chunky Pork Ribs in Sherry Garlic Marinade.
ABOVE LEFT: Italian-Style Pork Steaks with Prosciutto.
ABOVE: Pork and Noodle Salad.

Left: Serving ware and glasses from Freedom Furniture Stores. Above: Pottery from Kenwick Galleries.

VEGETABLES & SALADS

Simply by adding one or two of our interesting salads, vegetable dishes and accompaniments, you will make your party even more delicious for your guests. There are lots of ideas here, some light, some very hearty, all with inventive flavour combinations that will mix and match perfectly with any main course.

BEETROOT SALAD WITH BLUE CHEESE DRESSING

6 bacon rashers, chopped
300g snow peas
4 medium beetroot, coarsely grated
2 cups (80g) snow pea sprouts
1 medium avocado, sliced

BLUE CHEESE DRESSING
100g blue cheese
½ cup (125ml) sour cream
1 tablespoon tarragon vinegar
⅓ cup (80ml) cream
1 tablespoon water

Add bacon to hot pan, cook, stirring, until crisp; drain on absorbent paper. Boil, steam or microwave snow peas until just tender; drain, rinse under cold water, drain. Combine snow peas, beetroot, sprouts and avocado in bowl; mix gently. Sprinkle with bacon, drizzle with blue cheese dressing.

Blue Cheese Dressing: Blend or process cheese, sour cream and vinegar until combined. Transfer mixture to small bowl, stir in cream and water.

Serves 10.

- Dressing can be made a day ahead.
- Storage: Covered, in refrigerator.
- Freeze: Not suitable.
- Microwave: Snow peas suitable.

NEW POTATO AND BEAN SALAD WITH TAHINI SAUCE

2kg baby new potatoes
700g green beans, halved
400g feta cheese
½ cup (65g) drained chopped sun-dried tomatoes
2 tablespoons chopped fresh parsley

TAHINI SAUCE
¼ cup (60ml) tahini paste
1 tablespoon lemon juice
1 cup (250ml) plain yogurt
2 cloves garlic, crushed
¼ cup (60ml) water
¼ cup chopped fresh parsley

Boil, steam or microwave potatoes and beans separately until just tender; drain, rinse under cold water, drain. Cut cheese into 2cm cubes. Combine potatoes, beans and cheese in large bowl, add half the tahini sauce; mix gently. Drizzle with remaining sauce, sprinkle with tomatoes and parsley.

Tahini Sauce: Blend or process all ingredients until smooth.

Serves 10.

- Recipe can be made a day ahead.
- Storage: Covered, in refrigerator.
- Freeze: Not suitable.
- Microwave: Potatoes and beans suitable.

RIGHT: From left: Beetroot Salad with Blue Cheese Dressing, New Potato and Bean Salad with Tahini Sauce.

China from Johnson Brothers; tray from Freedom Furniture Stores; salad server from Accoutrement.

GINGER AND BOK CHOY NOODLE SALAD

375g packet fresh thin egg noodles
400g broccoli, chopped
150g sugar snap peas
1 medium red pepper
1 medium yellow pepper
150g oyster mushrooms
1 tablespoon light olive oil
1 bunch (about 750g) bok
**   choy, shredded**
1 cup (80g) bean sprouts
1 tablespoon grated fresh ginger
½ cup (125ml) light olive oil, extra
⅓ cup (80ml) light soy sauce
1 tablespoon white vinegar

Add noodles to pan of boiling water, boil, uncovered, until just tender; drain, rinse under cold water, drain. Boil, steam or microwave broccoli and peas separately until just tender; drain, rinse under cold water, drain. Cut peppers into very thin strips. Cut mushrooms in half lengthways.

Heat oil in pan, add bok choy, cook, stirring, until wilted; cool. Combine noodles, vegetables and sprouts in large bowl; mix well. Pour over combined ginger, extra oil, sauce and vinegar; mix well.

Serves 10.

- Recipe can be made a day ahead.
- Storage: Covered, in refrigerator.
- Freeze: Not suitable.
- Microwave: Noodles, broccoli and sugar snap peas suitable.

BEST PASTA SALAD

500g bow tie pasta
4 bacon rashers
2 medium red peppers
1 cup (110g) drained
**   sun-dried tomatoes**
1 tablespoon light olive oil
250g mozzarella cheese, chopped
½ cup (80g) pine nuts, toasted
2 tablespoons chopped fresh oregano
¼ cup chopped fresh chives
250g cherry tomatoes, halved

DRESSING
⅓ cup (80ml) olive oil
2 tablespoons white vinegar
1 teaspoon sugar
1 tablespoon balsamic vinegar
1 clove garlic, crushed
2 teaspoons French mustard

Add pasta to pan of boiling water, boil, uncovered, until tender; drain, rinse under cold water, drain well.

Cut bacon, peppers and tomatoes into thin strips. Heat oil in pan, add bacon, pepper and tomatoes, cook, stirring, until peppers are soft; cool. Combine pasta, pepper mixture, cheese, nuts, herbs and tomatoes in bowl, add dressing; mix well.
Dressing: Combine all ingredients in jar; shake well.

Serves 10.

- Salad can be made 3 hours ahead.
- Storage: Covered, in refrigerator.
- Freeze: Not suitable.
- Microwave: Suitable.

SPINACH, PEAR AND ASPARAGUS SALAD

2 bunches (about 500g)
**   fresh asparagus**
2 bunches (about 1.3kg)
**   English spinach**
2 firm pears, cored, sliced
2 nashi pears, cored, sliced
2 cups (200g) pecans or walnuts
200g goats' cheese, chopped

DRESSING
½ cup (125ml) olive oil
⅓ cup (80ml) lemon juice
1 teaspoon sugar
1 teaspoon French mustard
1 teaspoon seasoned pepper

Cut asparagus in half, add to pan of boiling water, simmer 30 seconds; drain, rinse under cold water, drain well. Combine asparagus, torn spinach leaves, both pears, nuts and cheese in bowl.

Just before serving, drizzle with dressing.
Dressing: Combine all ingredients in jar; shake well.

Serves 10.

- Recipe can be prepared 3 hours ahead.
- Storage: Covered, separately, in refrigerator.
- Freeze: Not suitable.
- Microwave: Asparagus suitable.

ABOVE: Ginger and Bok Choy Noodle Salad.
RIGHT: From back: Spinach, Pear and Asparagus Salad, Best Pasta Salad.

Above: Serving ware from Freedom Furniture Stores; salad servers from Accoutrement.
Right: Bowls, serviette rings and wire basket from Freedom Furniture Stores.

WARM BRAISED LEEK AND TOMATO SALAD

10 medium leeks
2 tablespoons olive oil
2 cloves garlic, crushed
¾ cup (180ml) chicken stock
¼ cup (60ml) olive oil, extra
1 tablespoon chopped fresh thyme
1 tablespoon chopped fresh oregano
1 clove garlic, extra
500g cherry tomatoes, halved
1 cup (160g) pitted black olives
1 tablespoon lemon juice

Using only white part of leeks, cut leeks lengthways into quarters. Heat oil in large pan, add leeks and garlic, cook, stirring, 3 minutes. Add stock, cook, covered, about 20 minutes, stirring occasionally, or until leeks are soft; drain, discard stock.

Combine extra oil, herbs and extra garlic in small bowl. Heat 2 tablespoons of herb mixture in pan, add tomatoes, cook, stirring, until tomatoes are soft. Combine leeks, tomato mixture, olives and juice in bowl; drizzle with remaining herb mixture.

Serves 10.

■ Recipe best made just before serving.
■ Freeze: Not suitable.
■ Microwave: Not suitable.

HERBED POLENTA SLICE

1 litre (4 cups) chicken stock
1 litre (4 cups) water
3 cups (450g) polenta
2 cloves garlic, crushed
2 egg yolks
2 tablespoons chopped fresh thyme
2 tablespoons chopped fresh chives
2 cups (160g) grated
parmesan cheese
40g butter, melted

Grease 2 x 20cm x 30cm lamington pans, cover bases with paper, grease paper. Bring stock and water to boil in pan, gradually add polenta, cook, stirring, about 5 minutes or until polenta is soft and thick; cool 2 minutes. Stir in garlic, egg yolks, herbs and half the cheese; mix well.

Spread mixture evenly into prepared pans, cover, refrigerate 2 hours or until firm. Turn out polenta, cut into pieces. Place polenta on greased oven trays, brush with butter, sprinkle with remaining cheese. Bake, uncovered, in moderately hot oven about 40 minutes or until lightly browned and heated through.

Makes about 30.

■ Polenta can be prepared 3 days ahead.
■ Storage: Covered, in refrigerator.
■ Freeze: Suitable before baking.
■ Microwave: Not suitable.

WARM ROASTED TOMATO AND ONION SALAD

1.5kg medium egg tomatoes
30 (about 750g) baby onions, peeled
30 cloves (about 2 bulbs)
garlic, peeled
2/3 cup (160ml) olive oil
2 teaspoons sambal oelek
1 tablespoon sugar
2 tablespoons bottled pesto
1 teaspoon salt
2 tablespoons balsamic vinegar
2 tablespoons chopped fresh oregano
1/2 cup shredded fresh basil
1/2 cup (80g) pine nuts, toasted

Cut tomatoes in half lengthways. Place tomatoes, cut side up, in large baking dish, add onions and garlic; drizzle with combined oil, sambal oelek, sugar, pesto and salt. Bake, uncovered, in hot oven about 30 minutes or until tomatoes are soft. Remove tomatoes from dish. Return onions and garlic to very hot oven for further 10 minutes or until onions are soft. Add vinegar, herbs and nuts to onion mixture; mix well. Spoon onion mixture over tomatoes; serve warm or cold.

Serves 10.

- Recipe can be made a day ahead.
- Storage: Covered, in refrigerator.
- Freeze: Not suitable.
- Microwave: Not suitable.

SALAD LEAVES WITH HORSERADISH DRESSING

3 bunches (about 750g)
fresh asparagus
2 medium witlof
2 bunches (about 300g) rocket
1 large green oak leaf lettuce
250g yellow teardrop tomatoes

CARAMELISED ONIONS
20 (about 500g) baby onions
1/2 cup (125ml) water
30g butter, chopped
1/4 cup (55g) sugar

HORSERADISH DRESSING
2 teaspoons Dijon mustard
2 teaspoons sugar
1 1/2 tablespoons prepared
horseradish
2 tablespoons white wine vinegar
1/2 cup (125ml) olive oil

Boil, steam or microwave asparagus until tender; drain, rinse under cold water, drain. Remove leaves from witlof, trim ends. Combine asparagus, witlof, rocket, torn lettuce leaves, tomatoes and caramelised onions in large bowl, add horseradish dressing; mix gently.
Caramelised Onions: Combine all ingredients in shallow pan, cook, covered, over low heat about 10 minutes or until onions are soft. Cook, uncovered, until liquid evaporates and onions are glazed.
Dressing: Combine all ingredients in jar; shake well.

Serves 10.

- Caramelised onions and horseradish dressing can be made a day ahead.
- Storage: Covered, separately, in refrigerator.
- Freeze: Not suitable.
- Microwave: Asparagus suitable.

LEFT: From left: Warm Braised Leek and Tomato Salad, Herbed Polenta Slice.
ABOVE: From left: Warm Roasted Tomato and Onion Salad, Salad Leaves with Horseradish Dressing.

Left: Plates, bowls, jug and salad servers from Accoutrement; wooden mats and glasses from Home & Garden on the Mall. Above: China and glassware from Freedom Furniture Stores.

EGGPLANT, KUMARA AND PEPPER SALAD

12 baby eggplants
400g kumara, peeled
1 tablespoon olive oil
1 medium red pepper, quartered
1 medium green pepper, quartered
½ cup (125ml) olive oil, extra
2 tablespoons balsamic vinegar
1 clove garlic, crushed
1 tablespoon honey
¼ cup (25g) drained chopped
** sun-dried tomatoes**
½ cup shredded fresh basil
¼ cup (40g) blanched almonds,
** toasted, chopped**
¼ cup (40g) pitted black olives,
** chopped**

Cut eggplants in half lengthways. Cut kumara into 1cm slices. Heat oil in griddle pan, add eggplants, kumara and peppers in batches, cook until browned.

Transfer vegetables to ovenproof serving dish, drizzle with extra oil, bake, covered, in moderate oven about 1 hour or until tender. Serve vegetables drizzled with combined vinegar, garlic and honey; top with combined remaining ingredients. Serve warm or cold.

Serves 10.

■ Recipe can be made a day ahead.
■ Storage: Covered, in refrigerator.
■ Freeze: Not suitable.
■ Microwave: Not suitable.

ARTICHOKE AND OLIVE SALAD

2 medium tomatoes
150g sliced pancetta
20 drained artichoke hearts, halved
1 cup (160g) pitted black olives
½ cup (75g) pimiento-stuffed
** green olives**
1 green oak leaf lettuce
1 red oak leaf lettuce

CROUTONS
½ loaf (350g) white bread
125g butter, melted
1 clove garlic, crushed
1 tablespoon chopped fresh chives
2 teaspoons chopped fresh oregano

DRESSING
2 tablespoons balsamic vinegar
½ cup (125ml) olive oil
1 teaspoon French mustard
½ teaspoon sugar

Cut tomatoes into thin wedges. Cut pancetta into thin strips. Combine tomatoes, pancetta, artichokes, olives, torn lettuce leaves, croutons and dressing in large bowl; mix well.
Croutons: Remove crusts from bread, cut bread into 2cm cubes. Place cubes in bowl, add combined butter, garlic and herbs; mix well. Place croutons in single layer on oven tray, toast, uncovered, in moderately hot oven about 20 minutes or until browned and crisp.

Dressing: Combine all ingredients in jar; shake well.

Serves 10.

■ Croutons can be made a day ahead.
■ Storage: Airtight container.
■ Freeze: Not suitable.
■ Microwave: Not suitable.

ORANGE AND LEAF SALAD WITH OLIVE CROUTES

1 radicchio lettuce
1 coral lettuce
1 green oak leaf lettuce
50g snow pea sprouts
5 medium oranges, segmented

DRESSING
¼ cup (60ml) orange juice
2 teaspoons grated fresh ginger
½ cup (125ml) orange juice, extra
¼ cup (60ml) olive oil

OLIVE CROUTES
1 large French bread stick
⅓ cup (80ml) olive paste
2 cloves garlic, crushed
3 teaspoons olive oil
2 teaspoons chopped fresh thyme

Combine torn lettuce leaves, sprouts and oranges in large bowl; drizzle with dressing. Serve with olive croutes.
Dressing: Heat juice and ginger in small pan, simmer, uncovered, until reduced by half; cool. Stir in extra juice and oil.
Olive Croutes: Cut bread into 1cm slices, spread 1 side with combined paste, garlic, oil and thyme. Place croutes in single layer on oven tray, toast, uncovered, in moderately hot oven about 8 minutes or until crisp.

Serves 10.

■ Croutes and dressing can be made 2 days ahead.
■ Storage: Croutes, airtight container. Dressing, covered, in refrigerator.
■ Freeze: Not suitable.
■ Microwave: Not suitable.

LEFT: Clockwise from left: Orange and Leaf Salad with Olive Croutes, Artichoke and Olive Salad, Eggplant, Kumara and Pepper Salad.

China from Johnson Brothers; clay bowl from Freedom Furniture Stores.

MARINATED MUSHROOM AND FENNEL SALAD

1 cup (250ml) light olive oil
1kg button mushrooms
4 small white onions
2 cloves garlic, crushed
2 medium red peppers
½ small fennel bulb, thinly sliced
1 tablespoon chopped fresh basil
1 cup (250ml) balsamic vinegar
¾ cup (180ml) dry red wine

CROUTONS
20 slices white bread
60g butter, melted

Heat ⅓ cup (80ml) of the oil in large pan, add a third of the mushrooms, cook, stirring, until just tender; remove from pan. Repeat with remaining oil and mushrooms in 2 batches.

Slice onions into thin rings. Add onions and garlic to same pan, cook, stirring, 4 minutes. Quarter peppers, remove seeds and membranes. Grill pepper, skin side up, until skin blisters and blackens. Peel away skin, slice peppers into thin strips. Combine mushrooms, onions, peppers and remaining ingredients in large bowl; mix well, cool. Serve with croutons.
Croutons: Use shaped cutters to cut croutons from each slice of bread. Brush bread with butter, grill until browned.

Serves 10.

- Recipe can be made a day ahead.
- Storage: Croutons, airtight container. Mushrooms, covered, in refrigerator.
- Freeze: Not suitable.
- Microwave: Not suitable.

BURGHUL SALAD WITH CITRUS DRESSING

3 cups (500g) burghul
2 small green cucumbers, peeled, seeded
coarse cooking salt
1 cup chopped fresh parsley
½ cup chopped fresh mint
3 medium avocados, chopped
3 medium tomatoes, chopped
3 medium oranges, segmented
18 drained artichoke hearts, halved

CITRUS DRESSING
1 cup (250ml) extra virgin olive oil
1 tablespoon grated orange rind
¼ cup (60ml) orange juice
½ cup (125ml) lemon juice
1 tablespoon Dijon mustard
1 tablespoon sugar
2 teaspoons ground cumin
1 teaspoon ground cinnamon
3 cloves garlic, crushed

Place burghul in heatproof bowl, cover with boiling water, stand 30 minutes. Drain burghul, squeeze out excess moisture. Chop cucumbers, sprinkle with salt, stand 30 minutes. Rinse cucumber under cold water; drain, pat dry with absorbent paper. Combine burghul, cucumber and remaining ingredients in large bowl, add citrus dressing; mix well.
Citrus Dressing: Combine all ingredients in jar; shake well.

Serves 10.

- Recipe can be made 3 hours ahead.
- Storage: Covered, in refrigerator.
- Freeze: Not suitable.

ABOVE: Marinated Mushroom and Fennel Salad
RIGHT: From left: Pea Salad with Pesto Croutons, Burghul Salad with Citrus Dressing.

Above: Plate from Home & Garden on the Mall; servers from Accoutrement.

PEA SALAD WITH PESTO CROUTONS

500g snow peas
300g sugar snap peas
160g snow pea sprouts

PESTO CROUTONS
½ loaf (350g) white bread
½ cup (125ml) olive oil
2 cloves garlic, crushed
2 tablespoons bottled pesto
1 teaspoon seasoned pepper

DRESSING
½ cup (125ml) olive oil
1 tablespoon seeded mustard
¼ cup (60ml) white vinegar
1 clove garlic, crushed
2 teaspoons brown sugar

Add both peas to pan of boiling water, simmer, uncovered, 30 seconds; drain, rinse under cold water, drain well. Combine both peas, sprouts, pesto croutons and dressing in bowl; mix gently.

Pesto Croutons: Remove crust from bread, cut bread into 2cm cubes. Combine bread cubes and remaining ingredients in bowl; mix well. Place croutons in single layer on oven tray. Bake, uncovered, in moderately hot oven about 15 minutes or until crisp.

Dressing: Combine all ingredients in jar; shake well.

Serves 10.

■ Pesto croutons and dressing can be made 2 days ahead.
■ Storage: Croutons, airtight container. Dressing, covered, in refrigerator.
■ Freeze: Not suitable.
■ Microwave: Both peas suitable.

FRUITY RICE

1¼ cups (230g) wild rice
⅓ cup (80ml) light olive oil
3 medium onions, sliced
1½ cups (300g) white long-grain rice
1.5 litres (6 cups) chicken stock
2 medium apples, peeled, cored
6 green shallots, chopped
1 cup (210g) chopped pitted prunes
⅓ cup (80ml) green ginger wine
¼ cup chopped fresh sage

Add wild rice to pan of boiling water, boil, uncovered, 20 minutes; drain.

Heat oil in pan, add onions, cook, stirring, until just soft. Add white rice, stir to coat rice with oil. Add stock and wild rice, simmer, uncovered, 8 minutes. Cut apples into 2cm pieces. Add apples and remaining ingredients to rice mixture, simmer further 6 minutes or until rice is tender and liquid absorbed.

Serves 10.

- Recipe best made close to serving.
- Freeze: Not suitable.
- Microwave: Suitable.

HOT CURRIED POTATO SALAD

2kg old potatoes

CURRY BUTTER
200g soft butter
1 tablespoon mild curry powder
1 tablespoon honey
½ teaspoon French mustard
1 teaspoon seeded mustard
1 tablespoon chopped
    fresh coriander
1 tablespoon chopped fresh chives

Wash potatoes well; chop unpeeled potatoes. Boil, steam or microwave potatoes until tender; drain well. Place hot potatoes in bowl, top with curry butter; mix gently.
Curry Butter: Beat butter, curry, honey and mustards together in bowl with electric mixer until fluffy; stir in herbs.

Serves 10.

- Curry butter can be made
  a day ahead.
- Storage: Covered, in refrigerator.
- Freeze: Curry butter suitable.
- Microwave: Potatoes suitable.

CHILLI HERB PASTA

700g spiral pasta
½ cup (125ml) olive oil
4 cloves garlic, crushed
1 teaspoon sambal oelek
⅔ cup chopped fresh chives
¾ cup chopped fresh parsley
¾ cup shredded fresh basil
⅓ cup chopped fresh thyme

Add pasta to large pan of boiling water, boil, uncovered, until just tender; drain.

Heat oil in large pan, add garlic and sambal oelek, cook, stirring, 1 minute. Stir in pasta and herbs; mix gently. Serve hot or cold.

Serves 10.

- Recipe can be made 3 hours ahead.
- Storage: Covered, in refrigerator.
- Freeze: Not suitable.
- Microwave: Pasta suitable.

POTATO BAKE WITH RED PEPPER SAUCE

9 large potatoes, peeled, chopped
140g butter, chopped
¼ teaspoon ground nutmeg
2 tablespoons cream
4 eggs, lightly beaten
2½ cups (310g) grated
    gruyere cheese

RED PEPPER SAUCE
4 medium red peppers
½ cup (40g) grated parmesan cheese
2 cloves garlic, chopped
½ cup (80g) pine nuts, toasted
½ cup (55g) drained
    sun-dried tomatoes
2 egg yolks
1 cup (70g) stale breadcrumbs
pinch cayenne pepper

Grease shallow ovenproof dish (3.5 litre/14 cup capacity). Boil, steam or microwave potatoes until tender; drain. Mash potatoes. Combine warm potato, butter, nutmeg, cream and eggs in large bowl; mix well until butter is melted. Spread half the potato mixture over base of prepared dish, top with red pepper sauce, then remaining potato mixture; sprinkle with cheese. Bake, uncovered, in moderately hot oven about 1 hour or until heated through and cheese is melted.

Red Pepper Sauce: Quarter peppers, remove seeds and membranes. Grill peppers, skin side up, until skin blisters and blackens. Peel away skin, chop peppers. Blend or process peppers and remaining ingredients until smooth.

Serves 10.

■ Recipe can be made a day ahead.
■ Storage: Covered, in refrigerator.
■ Freeze: Not suitable.
■ Microwave: Potatoes suitable.

ABOVE LEFT: From left: Hot Curried Potato Salad, Fruity Rice.
ABOVE: From back: Potato Bake with Red Pepper Sauce, Chilli Herb Pasta.

Above left: China from Royal Doulton; serving spoons, cane platter and serviettes from Accoutrement. Above: China, serving spoons and serviettes from Accoutrement.

BLACK-EYED BEAN AND RICE SALAD

2 cups (400g) black-eyed beans
3 cloves garlic
4cm piece of ginger, peeled
1 bay leaf
3 cups (750ml) water
12 saffron threads
2 cups (400g) long-grain rice
400g speck, chopped
8 green shallots, sliced
2 medium red peppers,
    finely chopped

DRESSING
1 cup (250ml) extra virgin olive oil
½ cup (125ml) white wine vinegar
pinch cayenne pepper

Cover beans with cold water in bowl, cover, stand overnight.

Add drained beans, garlic, thinly sliced ginger and bay leaf to pan of boiling water, simmer, uncovered, about 20 minutes or until tender; drain, rinse under cold water, drain. Discard bay leaf, reserve ginger and garlic for dressing.

Combine the water and saffron in pan, bring to boil, add rice, cook, covered, over very low heat 15 minutes. Remove from heat; cool. Add speck to dry pan, cook, stirring, until browned; drain on absorbent paper, cool. Combine beans, rice, speck, shallots and peppers in large bowl, add dressing; mix well.

Dressing: Blend or process all ingredients with reserved garlic and ginger until combined.

Serves 10.

- Recipe can be made 3 hours ahead.
- Storage: Covered, in refrigerator.
- Freeze: Not suitable.
- Microwave: Not suitable.

ORIENTAL CABBAGE SALAD

40g Chinese dried mushrooms
1 small Chinese cabbage, shredded
80g snow pea sprouts
227g can water chestnuts,
    drained, sliced
425g can baby corn, drained,
    quartered
1 long thin green cucumber,
    seeded, sliced
¼ cup (35g) sesame seeds, toasted
2 tablespoons black sesame seeds
½ cup chopped fresh coriander

DRESSING
⅓ cup (80ml) light soy sauce
½ cup (125ml) balsamic vinegar
¼ cup (60ml) sweet sake
1½ tablespoons sesame oil
½ cup (125ml) light olive oil
1½ teaspoons wasabi paste
¼ cup (70g) drained chopped
    pickled ginger

Place mushrooms in heatproof bowl, cover with boiling water, stand 20 minutes; drain. Discard stems, slice caps. Combine mushrooms with remaining ingredients in bowl, add dressing; mix well.
Dressing: Combine all ingredients in jar; shake well.

Serves 10.

- Recipe can be prepared a day ahead.
- Storage: Cabbage mixture and dressing, covered, separately, in refrigerator.
- Freeze: Not suitable.

ABOVE: Black-Eyed Bean and Rice Salad.
RIGHT: From left: Cauliflower, Anchovy and Olive Salad, Oriental Cabbage Salad.

Above: China from Primex Products. Right: China from Johnson Brothers; glasses and tray from Freedom Furniture Stores.

CAULIFLOWER, ANCHOVY AND OLIVE SALAD

1½ medium cauliflowers, chopped
1 cup (160g) pitted chopped
    black olives
½ cup (80g) pitted chopped
    green olives
½ cup (90g) drained capers
1 medium red Spanish onion,
    finely chopped
½ cup chopped fresh
    flat-leafed parsley
2 tablespoons chopped fresh basil

ANCHOVY DRESSING
56g can anchovy fillets, drained,
    chopped
⅓ cup (80ml) lemon juice
¼ cup (60ml) balsamic vinegar
2 cloves garlic, crushed
1¼ cups (310ml) olive oil

Boil, steam or microwave cauliflower until just tender; drain, rinse under cold water, drain well. Combine cauliflower with remaining ingredients in bowl, add dressing; mix well.
Anchovy Dressing: Combine all ingredients in jar; shake well.

Serves 10.

- Recipe can be made a day ahead.
- Storage: Covered, in refrigerator.
- Freeze: Not suitable.
- Microwave: Cauliflower suitable.

SPICY KUMARA AND POTATO

1kg kumara, peeled, chopped
600g potatoes, peeled, chopped
¼ cup (60ml) light olive oil
2 medium onions, sliced
4 cloves garlic, crushed
2 teaspoons ground cumin
2 teaspoons ground coriander
½ teaspoon turmeric
1 cup (250ml) coconut cream
1 teaspoon cumin seeds
2 small fresh red chillies, chopped

Boil, steam or microwave kumara and potatoes separately until just tender; drain. Heat oil in pan, add onions and garlic, cook, stirring, until onions are soft. Add spices, cook, stirring, until fragrant. Add kumara, potatoes and coconut cream, simmer, stirring, 2 minutes. Stir in seeds and chillies, simmer, uncovered, until mixture is thickened.

Serves 10.

◼ Recipe can be made a day ahead.
◼ Storage: Covered, in refrigerator.
◼ Freeze: Not suitable.
◼ Microwave: Kumara and potato suitable.

ABOVE: Spicy Kumara and Potato.

Above: Candlestick, rack and cane platter from Accoutrement.

LEMONY CARROT AND ZUCCHINI STICKS

6 medium carrots
7 medium zucchini

LEMON DRESSING
½ cup (125ml) mayonnaise
1 teaspoon grated lemon rind
2 tablespoons lemon juice
1 clove garlic, crushed
¼ cup (60ml) plain yogurt
2 tablespoons milk
2 tablespoons chopped fresh thyme
2 teaspoons French mustard

Cut carrots and zucchini into thin sticks. Add carrots to pan of boiling water, simmer, uncovered, 1 minute; drain, rinse under cold water, drain well. Combine carrots and zucchini in bowl; drizzle with lemon dressing.

Lemon Dressing: Whisk all ingredients in small bowl until combined.

Serves 10.

- Vegetables and dressing can be prepared a day ahead.
- Storage: Covered, separately, in refrigerator.
- Freeze: Not suitable.
- Microwave: Carrots suitable.

ABOVE: From left: Curried Couscous and Vegetable Salad, Lemony Carrot and Zucchini Sticks.

Above: Bowls, plates and rug from Barbara's Storehouse; glasses and serviettes from Home & Garden on the Mall; bottle and spoon from Accoutrement.

CURRIED COUSCOUS AND VEGETABLE SALAD

3 cups (750ml) vegetable stock
2 cups (300g) couscous
1 medium carrot
1 medium red pepper
1 medium green pepper
1 medium yellow pepper
1 medium apple
60g butter
1 medium onion, sliced
2 teaspoons curry powder
1 teaspoon ground cumin

DRESSING
¼ cup (60ml) lime juice
½ cup (125ml) olive oil
1 teaspoon sugar
¼ cup (60ml) coconut milk

Bring stock to boil in pan, stir in couscous, return to boil; remove pan from heat. Cover, stand 10 minutes.

Cut carrot, peppers and apple into thin strips. Heat butter in pan, add carrot, peppers, apple, onion, curry powder and cumin, cook, stirring, until onion is soft. Combine couscous, vegetable mixture and dressing in bowl. Serve warm.

Dressing: Combine all ingredients in jar; shake well.

Serves 10.

- Salad and dressing can be prepared a day ahead.
- Storage: Covered, separately, in refrigerator.
- Freeze: Not suitable.
- Microwave: Suitable.

DESSERTS & PETITS FOURS

Guests always love a truly special dessert, and we have some beauties, plus irresistible petits fours to serve with coffee. Here you'll find a lavish choice, with tastes and textures to tempt everyone, and most can be made ahead so they are in the refrigerator, ready for serving. We have included a sumptuous, triple-chocolate cake based on a packet mix, plus a big rich fruit cake where all the ingredients go into one bowl for extra-easy mixing.

SUMMER BERRY TRIFLE

350g sponge cake
¼ cup (60ml) Grand Marnier
500g strawberries
1 tablespoon icing sugar mixture
400g blueberries
400g raspberries
½ cup (50g) walnuts,
**   toasted, chopped**

VANILLA CUSTARD
½ cup (110g) sugar
8 egg yolks
1½ tablespoons cornflour
1½ tablespoons water
2 cups (500ml) milk
1 teaspoon vanilla essence
¼ cup (60ml) cream

Cut sponge into 2cm pieces, place in large dish (3 litre/12 cup capacity). Sprinkle with liqueur; stand 20 minutes. Blend or process half the strawberries and icing sugar until smooth, pour over sponge. Top with a layer of blueberries, raspberries and remaining strawberries. Pour over vanilla custard. Cover, refrigerate 1 hour. Serve summer berry trifle sprinkled with nuts.

Vanilla Custard: Beat sugar and yolks in small bowl with electric mixer until thick and creamy, stir in blended cornflour and water. Heat milk and essence in pan, bring to boil, remove from heat, cool 2 minutes. Stir milk into egg mixture. Return mixture to pan, stir over low heat until custard boils and thickens; cool. Cover, refrigerate until cold; stir in cream.

Serves 10.

- Vanilla custard can be made a day ahead. Recipe can be made 3 hours ahead.
- Storage: Covered, in refrigerator.
- Freeze: Not suitable.
- Microwave: Not suitable.

RIGHT: Summer Berry Trifle.

Bowl and glasses from Bohemia Crystal Shop.

RICOTTA CAKE WITH PRUNE ICE-CREAM

2 cups (300g) plain flour
1 cup (150g) self-raising flour
⅔ cup (130g) firmly packed brown sugar
1 cup (125g) packaged ground almonds
1 egg, lightly beaten
250g butter, chopped

FILLING
2 tablespoons pine nuts, toasted
2 tablespoons blanched almonds, toasted
⅓ cup (75g) castor sugar
1 tablespoon water
800g ricotta cheese
2 tablespoons dark rum
50g dark chocolate, finely chopped
1 cup (220g) castor sugar, extra

PRUNE ICE-CREAM
1½ cups (255g) pitted prunes
1 cup (250ml) boiling water
2 litres vanilla ice-cream
2 tablespoons port
¼ cup (40g) pitted prunes, chopped, extra

Grease 23cm springform tin, cover base with foil. Blend or process flours, sugar, nuts and egg in 2 batches until combined. Add butter in 2 batches, blend or process until mixture resembles fine breadcrumbs.

Press half the nut mixture over base of prepared tin, top with filling, spoon over remaining nut mixture. Place tin on oven tray, bake in moderate oven about 1 hour; cool in tin. Cover, refrigerate overnight. Serve with prune ice-cream.

Filling: Spread both nuts evenly onto greased oven tray. Combine sugar and water in small pan, stir over heat, without boiling, until sugar is dissolved, then simmer, without stirring, until syrup is caramel in colour. Allow bubbles to subside, pour evenly over nuts. Stand until set, break into pieces, blend or process until finely crushed. Blend or process cheese until smooth. Transfer to bowl, stir in nut mixture, rum, chocolate and extra sugar.

Prune Ice-Cream: Place prunes in heatproof bowl, cover with the boiling water, stand 1 hour. Add undrained prunes to pan, bring to boil, simmer, uncovered, about 5 minutes or until liquid is absorbed and mixture pulpy; cool. Beat ice-cream in large bowl with electric mixer until soft. Add prune mixture, port and extra prunes, beat on low speed until combined. Spread mixture into 14cm x 21cm loaf pan, cover, freeze until firm.

Serves 10.
■ Recipe best made a day ahead.
■ Storage: Ricotta cake, covered, in refrigerator. Ice-cream, covered, in freezer.
■ Freeze: Cake not suitable.
■ Microwave: Prunes suitable.

SHORTBREAD STRAWBERRY HEARTS

2 tablespoons rice flour
2 tablespoons icing sugar mixture
2 tablespoons cornflour
1 cup (150g) plain flour
125g butter, chopped
3 teaspoons water, approximately
300ml sour cream
125g strawberries, quartered

Sift dry ingredients into bowl, rub in butter. Add enough water to make ingredients cling together, cover, refrigerate 30 minutes.

Cut dough in half, roll each half between greaseproof paper until 3mm thick. Cut out 5cm heart shapes, place about 3cm apart on oven trays covered with baking paper. Bake in moderately slow oven about 25 minutes or until lightly browned. Stand 5 minutes before lifting onto wire racks to cool. Top with sour cream and strawberries. Dust with sifted icing sugar, if desired.

Make about 60.
■ Shortbread hearts can be made a week ahead.
■ Storage: Airtight container.
■ Freeze: Shortbread suitable without cream and strawberries.
■ Microwave: Not suitable.

LEFT: Ricotta Cake with Prune Ice-Cream.
BELOW: Shortbread Strawberry Hearts.

Left: China from Waterford Wedgwood; cutlery from The Bay Tree Kitchen Shop; cake server from Linen & Lace of Balmain. Below: China from Waterford Wedgwood; glass basket from Home & Garden on the Mall.

MANGO ICE-CREAM CAKE WITH CARAMEL MANGOES

5 egg whites
¼ cup (55g) castor sugar
¾ cup (120g) icing sugar mixture
1⅓ cups (120g) coconut
100g (⅔ cup) Choc Melts, melted

MANGO ICE-CREAM
4 medium (about 2.4kg) mangoes
⅔ cup (160ml) milk
300ml cream
6 egg yolks
½ cup (110g) castor sugar
1 tablespoon Grand Marnier

CARAMEL MANGOES
125g butter, chopped
½ cup (100g) firmly packed brown sugar
4 medium mangoes (about 2.4kg), sliced

Grease 2 oven trays, cover with baking paper, mark 24cm circles on paper. Beat egg whites in bowl with electric mixer until soft peaks form; add castor sugar gradually, beat until dissolved between additions. Beat in sifted icing sugar in 2 batches; gently fold in coconut in 2 batches.

Divide mixture between the 2 circles, smooth with spatula. Bake in moderate oven about 25 minutes or until meringues are firm to touch.

Lightly oil deep 25cm round cake pan (or springform tin), cover base and side with plastic wrap.

Place a meringue disc in prepared cake pan, pour mango ice-cream over meringue, top with remaining meringue disc; cover, freeze until firm.

Measure a strip of baking paper to fit around side of cake, spread evenly with chocolate; do not allow to set. Turn cake onto serving plate, wrap chocolate ribbon around side of cake; return to freezer until set. Peel away paper, serve mango ice-cream cake with caramel mangoes.

Mango Ice-Cream: Blend or process mangoes until smooth. Combine milk and cream in small pan, bring to boil, remove from heat. Beat egg yolks and sugar in medium bowl with electric mixer until thick and creamy, beat in mango puree and liqueur. Gradually beat in hot milk mixture; cool. Pour mixture into lamington pans, cover, freeze until firm. Remove ice-cream from pans, beat in large bowl with electric mixer until thick.

Caramel Mangoes: Combine butter and sugar in large heavy-based pan, stir over heat, without boiling, until sugar is dissolved. Simmer mixture, uncovered, without stirring, 1 minute, add mangoes, simmer further 5 minutes or until caramel is thickened slightly.

Serves 10.

- Cake can be made a week ahead. Caramel mangoes can be made a day ahead.
- Storage: Cake, covered, in freezer. Caramel mangoes, covered, in refrigerator.
- Freezer: Caramel mangoes not suitable.
- Microwave: Not suitable.

BABY PAVLOVAS WITH MIXED BERRIES

6 egg whites
1½ cups (330g) castor sugar
1½ tablespoons cornflour
1½ teaspoons lemon juice
600ml thickened cream
2 tablespoons icing sugar mixture
2 tablespoons Grand Marnier
250g strawberries, halved
200g raspberries
200g blueberries
200g boysenberries

Cover 3 oven trays with foil, grease foil, dust with flour, mark 10 x 10cm circles on foil. Beat egg whites in large bowl with electric mixer until soft peaks form. Gradually add sugar, beating until dissolved between additions. Fold in blended cornflour and juice.

Spread 2 level tablespoons of mixture over each circle. Spoon remaining mixture into piping bag fitted with a small star tube. Pipe around edge of circles to form baskets. Bake in very slow oven about 1 hour or until meringue is dry to touch. Cool pavlovas in oven with door ajar.

Combine cream, sifted icing sugar and liqueur in bowl, beat until soft peaks form. Fill pavlovas with cream mixture, top with mixed berries.

Makes 10.

- Meringues can be made a week ahead.
- Storage: Airtight container.
- Freeze: Not suitable.
- Microwave: Not suitable.

LEFT: Mango Ice-Cream Cake with Caramel Mangoes.
RIGHT: Baby Pavlovas with Mixed Berries.

Left: China from The Bay Tree Kitchen Shop.
Right: China from Bohemia Crystal Shop; forks from Home & Garden on the Mall.

RASPBERRY AND VANILLA SORBET TERRINE

1⅓ cups (330ml) water
1½ cups (330g) sugar
500g raspberries

VANILLA ICE-CREAM
2 vanilla beans
2 cups (500ml) milk
2 cups (500ml) cream
8 egg yolks
1 cup (220g) castor sugar

BLACKCURRANT SAUCE
750g frozen blackcurrants, thawed
¼ cup (60ml) Cassis

Line 11cm x 25cm (1.5 litre/6 cup capacity) loaf dish with plastic wrap; place in freezer. Combine water and sugar in pan, stir over heat, without boiling, until sugar is dissolved, simmer, without stirring, 1 minute; cool. You need about 2 cups (500ml) sugar syrup.

Push raspberries through fine strainer, discard seeds. You need 1⅓ cups (330ml) puree. Combine puree and 1¼ cups (310ml) of the sugar syrup in bowl. Freeze raspberry mixture in ice-cream maker according to manufacturer's instructions.

Place a third of the raspberry sorbet in cake pan, cover, freeze. Place remaining sorbet on large piece of foil, roll into 25cm log, twist ends to secure, freeze 2 hours or until firm.

Spoon half the vanilla ice-cream into prepared dish. Remove foil from log, press log firmly into ice-cream. Spoon remaining ice-cream over and around log to completely seal with ice-cream; freeze until firm.

Using palette knife and damp pastry brush, spread a quarter of reserved raspberry sorbet in a thin, even layer over ice-cream in dish, cover, freeze until firm. Turn terrine onto plate, spread remaining sorbet over terrine, cover, freeze until firm. Serve terrine with blackcurrant sauce.

Vanilla Ice-Cream: Split vanilla beans lengthways, remove and reserve seeds. Combine beans, reserved seeds, milk and cream in pan, bring to boil, remove from heat; cover, stand 30 minutes.

Whisk egg yolks and sugar in large bowl until creamy, gradually whisk in milk mixture. Pour mixture back into same pan, stir over heat, without boiling, until mixture thickens slightly, strain; cool. Freeze mixture in ice-cream maker according to manufacturer's instructions.

Blackcurrant Sauce: Blend or process blackcurrants until smooth, strain; discard seeds. Combine puree, ⅔ cup (160ml) of reserved sugar syrup and liqueur in bowl. Cover, refrigerate.

Serves 10.

■ Terrine can be made a week ahead. Sauce can be made 4 days ahead.
■ Storage: Terrine, covered, in freezer. Sauce, covered, in refrigerator.
■ Freeze: Sauce not suitable.
■ Microwave: Not suitable.

CHOCOLATE MOUSSE CAKE WITH COFFEE ANGLAISE

6 eggs, separated
½ cup (80g) icing sugar mixture
¼ cup (25g) cocoa
2 tablespoons cornflour
150g dark chocolate, melted
1 tablespoon water
1 litre (4 cups) thickened cream
600g dark chocolate, melted, extra

COFFEE ANGLAISE
3 cups (750ml) milk
1½ cups (125g) coffee beans
8 egg yolks
¾ cup (165g) castor sugar

Grease 26cm x 32cm Swiss roll pan, cover base and sides with baking paper. Beat egg yolks and icing sugar mixture in small bowl with electric mixer until light and creamy. Transfer to large bowl. Fold in combined sifted cocoa and cornflour, then chocolate; stir in water.

Beat egg whites in small bowl with electric mixer until soft peaks form, fold into chocolate mixture in 2 batches. Spread mixture into prepared pan, bake in moderate oven about 15 minutes. Turn cake onto wire rack covered with baking paper; cool.

Cut out circle of cake large enough to fit 26cm springform tin, using smaller pieces to fit, if necessary. Beat cream in large bowl with electric mixer until slightly thickened. Fold in warm extra chocolate in 4 batches. Pour mixture over cake base, refrigerate until set. Remove cake from tin, dust with sifted extra cocoa, serve with coffee anglaise.

Coffee Anglaise: Combine milk and beans in pan, bring to boil, remove from heat, cover, stand 1 hour. Whisk egg yolks and sugar in large bowl, whisk in milk mixture. Return mixture to same pan, stir over heat, without boiling, until slightly thickened, strain; cool. Cover, refrigerate.

Serves 12.

■ Recipe can be made 2 days ahead.
■ Storage: Covered, separately, in refrigerator.
■ Freeze: Cake base suitable.
■ Microwave: Not suitable.

RIGHT: From back: Raspberry and Vanilla Sorbet Terrine, Chocolate Mousse Cake with Coffee Anglaise.

Plates, cake server and glasses from Waterford Wedgwood.

POACHED PEARS WITH PASTRY TWISTS

10 pears, peeled
1 litre (4 cups) dry red wine
2 cups (500ml) water
1¼ cups (275g) castor sugar
1 cinnamon stick
1 vanilla bean, split
2 strips lemon rind
2 strips orange rind
2 tablespoons lemon juice
⅓ cup (80ml) orange juice
2 tablespoons castor sugar, extra
2 tablespoons Cassis

PASTRY TWISTS
4 sheets ready-rolled puff pastry
1 egg white, lightly beaten
½ cup (110g) castor sugar
¼ cup (55g) castor sugar, extra

Core pears, using a melon baller; leave stems attached. Combine wine, water, sugar, cinnamon, vanilla, rinds and juices in large pan, stir over heat, without boiling, until sugar is dissolved. Add pears, simmer, covered, about 12 minutes or until pears are soft; remove from heat. Top with plastic wrap to keep pears submerged; cool. Refrigerate about 3 hours or until cold.

Remove pears from liquid; strain. Boil liquid in pan, uncovered, until reduced to 1½ cups (375ml), stir in extra sugar and liqueur. Stir over heat, without boiling, until sugar is dissolved, then simmer, uncovered, 2 minutes; cool. Cover, refrigerate until cold. Serve pears with the liqueur syrup and pastry twists.

Pastry Twists: Grease oven trays, cover with baking paper. Brush 2 sheets of pastry with some of the egg white.

Sprinkle 1 sheet with ¼ cup (55g) of the sugar, top with second sheet, egg white side down. Brush pastry with more egg white, sprinkle with 1 tablespoon of extra castor sugar.

Cut pastry in half lengthways, then into 2cm strips. Twist pastry, place on prepared trays, brush with more egg white, sprinkle with more extra sugar. Bake in hot oven about 12 minutes or until crisp. Repeat with remaining pastry, egg white, sugar and extra sugar.

Serves 10.

- ■ Recipe can be made a day ahead.
- ■ Storage: Pears, covered, in refrigerator. Pastry twists, in airtight container.
- ■ Freeze: Not suitable.
- ■ Microwave: Not suitable.

RICH MOCHA TRUFFLES

60g unsalted butter, melted
100g dark chocolate, melted
1½ teaspoons dry instant coffee
2 teaspoons hot water
⅔ cup (70g) chocolate cake crumbs
2 teaspoons Tia Maria or Kahlua
¾ cup (65g) coconut

Combine butter, chocolate, blended coffee and water, cake crumbs and liqueur in bowl; mix well. Refrigerate about 1 hour or until mixture is firm. Roll level teaspoons of mixture into balls, toss in coconut; refrigerate until firm. Serve truffles straight from refrigerator.

Makes about 45.

- Truffles can be made 2 weeks ahead.
- Storage: Covered, in refrigerator.
- Freeze: Suitable.
- Microwave: Butter and chocolate suitable.

ORANGE AND PINE NUT BISCOTTI

125g butter, chopped
1 tablespoon grated orange rind
¾ cup (165g) sugar
¼ teaspoon ground ginger
3 eggs
2 tablespoons Grand Marnier
1½ cups (225g) plain flour
¾ cup (110g) self-raising flour
⅔ cup (100g) pine nuts, toasted

Beat butter, rind, sugar and ginger in small bowl with electric mixer until light and fluffy. Add eggs 1 at a time, beating well after each addition. Stir in liqueur, then sifted flours and nuts, mix to a soft dough. Cover, refrigerate 1 hour.

Divide dough in half, shape each half into 5cm x 30cm log. Place logs on greased oven tray, bake, uncovered, in moderate oven about 20 minutes or until lightly browned. Remove from oven, cool on oven tray. Cut into 1cm slices with serrated knife. Place slices, cut side up, close together on greased oven trays, bake in moderate oven about 25 minutes or until dry and crisp.

Makes about 40.

- Biscotti can be made a week ahead.
- Storage: Airtight container.
- Freeze: Not suitable.
- Microwave: Not suitable.

LEFT: Poached Pears with Pastry Twists.
ABOVE: Clockwise from back: Orange and Pine Nut Biscotti, Coffee Meringue Kisses, Rich Mocha Truffles.

Left: China and glasses from Royal Doulton.
Above: China from The Design Store.

COFFEE MERINGUE KISSES

2 egg whites
½ cup (110g) castor sugar
2 teaspoons dry instant coffee
½ teaspoon hot water

COFFEE CREAM
50g soft butter
3 teaspoons thickened cream
1 teaspoon dry instant coffee
1 teaspoon water
¾ cup (120g) icing sugar mixture

Cover 2 oven trays with foil, grease foil, dust with flour, mark 3cm circles about 3cm apart on foil. Beat egg whites in small bowl with electric mixer until soft peaks form. Gradually add sugar, beating until dissolved between additions. Stir in combined coffee and water.

Spoon mixture into piping bag fitted with 1cm fluted tube, pipe mixture onto circles on prepared trays. You will need 40 meringues. Bake in very slow oven about 1½ hours or until meringues are firm to touch. Cool in oven with door ajar. Sandwich meringues with coffee cream.

Coffee Cream: Beat butter, cream, combined coffee and water and half the sifted icing sugar mixture in small bowl until smooth. Gradually beat in remaining icing sugar mixture.

Makes 20.

- Unfilled meringues can be made a day ahead.
- Storage: Airtight container.
- Freeze: Not suitable.
- Microwave: Not suitable.

STICKY BUTTERNUT FLAN

2¼ cups (335g) plain flour
185g butter
⅔ cup (80g) ground almonds
2 egg yolks
1½ tablespoons lemon juice,
  approximately

FILLING
½ cup (75g) hazelnuts,
  toasted, chopped
¾ cup (75g) pecans, chopped
½ cup (75g) macadamias,
  toasted, halved
½ cup (80g) almond kernels, chopped
1⅔ cups (330g) firmly packed
  brown sugar
1¼ cups (310ml) dark corn syrup
80g butter, melted

Grease 2 x 11cm x 35cm flan tins. Sift flour into bowl, rub in butter. Stir in nuts, egg yolks and enough juice to make ingredients cling together. Press dough into

ball, knead gently on lightly floured surface until smooth, cover, refrigerate 30 minutes.

Cut dough in half, roll each half until large enough to line prepared tins. Lift pastry into tins, ease into sides, trim edges. Cover pastry with greaseproof paper, fill with dried beans or rice. Place tins on oven tray, bake in moderately hot oven 10 minutes, remove paper and beans, bake further 10 minutes or until pastry is browned; cool.

Divide filling evenly between pastry cases. Bake, uncovered, in moderately slow oven 45 minutes; cool. Cover, refrigerate until cold.
Filling: Combine all ingredients in bowl; mix well.

Serves 10.

■ Recipe can be made a day ahead.
■ Storage: Covered, in refrigerator.
■ Freeze: Uncooked pastry suitable.
■ Microwave: Not suitable.

ALMOND SYRUP CAKE WITH COINTREAU ICE-CREAM

185g butter, chopped
2 teaspoons grated orange rind
1½ cups (330g) castor sugar
6 eggs
3 cups (375g) packaged
  ground almonds
1½ cups (225g) self-raising flour

ORANGE SYRUP
2 medium oranges
¾ cup (180ml) orange juice
1½ cups (330g) sugar
¼ cup (60ml) lemon juice

COINTREAU ICE-CREAM
2 litres vanilla ice-cream
⅓ cup (80ml) Cointreau

Grease deep 25cm round cake pan, cover base with paper; grease paper. Beat butter, rind and sugar in medium bowl with electric mixer until light and fluffy.

Beat in eggs 1 at a time, beat until combined. Transfer mixture to large bowl, stir in nuts and sifted flour in 2 batches.

Spread mixture into prepared pan, bake in moderately slow oven about 55 minutes. Pour ⅓ cup (80ml) of hot orange syrup over hot cake, stand 10 minutes before turning onto wire rack to cool. Serve cake with remaining orange syrup and Cointreau ice-cream.

Orange Syrup: Using vegetable peeler, peel rind thinly from oranges, cut into very thin strips. Combine rind with remaining ingredients in pan, stir over heat, without boiling, until sugar is dissolved, simmer, uncovered, without stirring, 3 minutes.

Cointreau Ice-Cream: Beat ice-cream in large bowl with electric mixer until soft, add liqueur, beat until combined. Spread mixture into deep pan (2.5 litre/10 cup capacity), cover, freeze until firm.

Serves 10 to 12.

- Cake and syrup can be made 2 days ahead. Ice-cream can be made a week ahead.
- Storage: Cake, in airtight container. Syrup, covered, in refrigerator. Ice-cream, covered, in freezer.
- Freeze: Cake and syrup suitable.
- Microwave: Not suitable.

TANGY LIME MOUSSE WITH ALMOND TUILLES

You need about 4 limes for this recipe.

2 tablespoons gelatine
¼ cup (60ml) water
6 eggs, separated
1½ cups (330g) castor sugar
1½ tablespoons grated lime rind
½ cup (125ml) lime juice
1 tablespoon Cointreau
600ml thickened cream
5 medium oranges, segmented

ALMOND TUILLES
2 egg whites
½ cup (110g) castor sugar
½ cup (75g) plain flour
60g butter, melted
1 tablespoon grated orange rind
¾ cup (60g) flaked almonds

CANDIED ORANGE RIND
5 medium oranges
1 cup (220g) sugar
2 cups (500ml) water

Sprinkle gelatine over water in cup, stand in pan of simmering water, stir until dissolved. Beat egg yolks, sugar and rind in large bowl with electric mixer until thick and pale. Beat in juice, liqueur and gelatine mixture; stand until partly set.

Beat cream in large bowl with electric mixer until soft peaks form; fold cream into lime mixture in 2 batches. Beat egg whites in small bowl with electric mixer until soft peaks form; fold into lime mixture in 2 batches.

Spoon mixture evenly into 10 oiled moulds (1 cup/250ml capacity); cover, refrigerate several hours or overnight. Turn mousses onto plates, serve with orange segments, almond tuilles and drained candied orange rind.

Almond Tuilles: Grease 2 oven trays. Beat egg whites in small bowl with electric mixer until soft peaks form, gradually add sugar, beat until dissolved. Gently fold in flour, butter and rind.

Spread 1 level tablespoon of mixture onto a prepared tray, spread to 10cm round; allow 4 tuilles per tray. Sprinkle with nuts. Bake tuilles in moderate oven about 5 minutes or until lightly browned. Remove carefully from tray with spatula while still warm. Shape quickly around rolling pin, leave to set. Repeat with remaining mixture and nuts.

Candied Rind: Using a vegetable peeler, peel rind thinly from oranges. Cut rind into thin strips. Place rind in pan, cover with water, bring to boil, drain; repeat twice.

Place sugar and the 2 cups of water in pan, stir over heat, without boiling, until sugar is dissolved, simmer 1 minute. Add rind, simmer, without stirring, about 10 minutes or until rind is clear; cool.

Serves 10.

- Mousse can be made a day ahead. Tuilles can be made a week ahead.
- Storage: Mousse, covered, in refrigerator. Tuilles, airtight container.
- Freeze: Not suitable.
- Microwave: Gelatine suitable.

LEFT: From back: Almond Syrup Cake with Cointreau Ice-Cream, Sticky Butternut Flan. BELOW: Tangy Lime Mousse with Almond Tuilles.

Below: China from Villeroy & Boch.

TIRAMISU TERRINE

**2 x 125g packets small sponge
  finger biscuits**
2 tablespoons dry instant coffee
⅔ cup (160ml) hot water
⅔ cup (160ml) marsala

FILLING
1 teaspoon gelatine
2 teaspoons water
2 egg yolks
½ cup (80g) icing sugar mixture
500g mascarpone cheese
½ cup (125ml) thickened cream

CHOCOLATE SAUCE
300ml thickened cream
100g dark chocolate, chopped
1 tablespoon Tia Maria or Kahlua
1 tablespoon icing sugar mixture

Grease 11cm x 25cm glass loaf dish
(1.5 litre/6 cup capacity), line with plastic
wrap. Quickly dip biscuits into combined
coffee, water and marsala. Line base and
long sides of prepared dish with biscuits;
trim biscuits to fit. Spoon filling into dish,
top with remaining biscuits; cover,
refrigerate several hours or overnight.
Serve with chocolate sauce.
Filling: Sprinkle gelatine over water in
cup, stand in pan of simmering water, stir
until dissolved. Beat egg yolks, sugar,
cheese and cream in small bowl with
electric mixer until mixture is thick; fold in
gelatine mixture.
Chocolate Sauce: Combine all ingredients in pan, whisk over heat, without boiling, until chocolate is melted and
mixture is smooth; cool.
- ■ Terrine and chocolate sauce can be
  made 2 days ahead.
- ■ Storage: Covered, separately,
  in refrigerator.
- ■ Freeze: Terrine suitable.
- ■ Microwave: Gelatine suitable.

FIG AND DATE TART

3 cups (450g) plain flour
¼ cup (40g) icing sugar mixture
280g butter, chopped
3 egg yolks
2 tablespoons milk, approximately
7 fresh figs, quartered
6 fresh dates, pitted, quartered

FILLING
1⅔ cups (410ml) cream
1 teaspoon vanilla essence
8 egg yolks
¼ cup (55g) castor sugar

Sift flour and sugar into large bowl, rub in
butter. Add egg yolks and enough milk to
form a soft dough. Turn dough onto
floured surface, knead until smooth,
cover, refrigerate 30 minutes.
Cut dough in half, roll each half on lightly floured surface until large enough to line
2 x 24cm flan tins. Lift pastry into tins,
ease into sides, trim edges. Place on oven
trays. Cover pastry with paper, fill with
dried beans or rice. Bake in moderately

hot oven 10 minutes. Remove paper and
beans, bake further 10 minutes or until
browned; cool.
Divide figs and dates between pastry
cases, top evenly with filling. Bake in
moderate oven about 55 minutes or until
firm. Serve warm or cold.
Filling: Combine cream and essence in
pan, bring to boil, remove from heat; cool
to room temperature.
Beat egg yolks and sugar in small bowl
with electric mixer until thick and creamy,
add strained cream mixture; beat well.

Serves 10.
- ■ Recipe can be made 3 hours ahead.
- ■ Storage: Covered, at room
  temperature.
- ■ Freeze: Not suitable.
- ■ Microwave: Cream suitable.

CHOCOLATE LIQUEUR TRUFFLES

300g dark chocolate, chopped
½ cup (125ml) cream
50g butter
1 tablespoon Grand Marnier
1 tablespoon dark rum
½ cup (50g) cocoa

CANDIED ORANGE RIND
1 medium orange
1 cup (250ml) water
1 cup (220g) sugar

Combine chocolate, cream and butter in
heatproof bowl, stir over pan of simmering
water until smooth. Divide mixture into 2

bowls. Stir liqueur into 1 bowl; stir rum into
other bowl. Refrigerate until set.
Using melon baller, scoop balls from
rum mixture, drop into bowl of cocoa, toss
to coat; cover, refrigerate. Just before
serving, shake away excess cocoa.
Stand liqueur mixture at room temperature until slightly softened. Spoon into
piping bag fitted with 1cm star tube, pipe
into foil cups, refrigerate until firm. Serve
topped with candied orange rind.
Candied Orange Rind: Using a vegetable peeler, peel rind thinly from orange.
Cut rind into very thin strips. Place rind in
pan, cover with cold water, bring to boil;
drain. Combine water and sugar in small
pan, stir over heat, without boiling, until
sugar is dissolved. Add rind, simmer,
without stirring, about 10 minutes or until
rind is clear; drain.

Makes about 50.
- ■ Recipe can be made a week ahead.
- ■ Storage: Covered, in refrigerator.
- ■ Freeze: Truffle mixture suitable.
- ■ Microwave: Chocolate mixture
  suitable.

*LEFT: From back: Tiramisu Terrine, Fig and
Date Tart.*
ABOVE: Chocolate Liqueur Truffles.

*Left: China, glassware, cloth and serviettes from
Waterford Wedgwood. Above: China from
Waterford Wedgwood.*

GLACE FRUIT BREAD

2 egg whites
¼ cup (55g) castor sugar
¾ cup (110g) plain flour
½ cup (80g) blanched almonds
¼ cup (50g) red glace
   cherries, chopped
2 glace apricots, chopped
2 glace pineapple rings, chopped
2 glace figs, chopped

Grease 8cm x 26cm bar cake pan. Beat egg whites in small bowl with electric mixer until soft peaks form, gradually add sugar, beat until dissolved. Fold in sifted flour, nuts and fruit; spread into prepared pan. Bake in moderate oven about 30 minutes or until lightly browned and skewer comes out clean when tested. Cool in pan, wrap in foil; stand overnight.

Cut bread into 3mm slices, using serrated knife. Place slices in single layer on oven trays covered with greased baking paper. Bake in slow oven about 25 minutes or until crisp and dry.

Makes about 60.

- Recipe can be made a week ahead.
- Storage: Airtight container.
- Freeze: Unsliced bread suitable.
- Microwave: Not suitable.

CHOCOLATE MARSHMALLOW FUDGE

2 x 100g packets white marshmallows
125g unsalted butter, chopped
2 tablespoons cream
2 x 200g blocks Toblerone
   chocolate, chopped
1 cup (140g) slivered
   almonds, toasted

Grease deep 19cm square cake pan, line base and sides with foil; grease foil. Combine marshmallows, butter and cream in pan, stir over low heat until marshmallows are melted. Remove from heat, add chocolate, stir until melted. Stir in nuts, spoon mixture into prepared pan; cool. Cover, refrigerate until set.

Serves 10.

- Recipe can be made a week ahead.
- Storage: Covered, in refrigerator.
- Freeze: Not suitable.
- Microwave: Not suitable.

LEFT: From back: Glace Fruit Bread, Chocolate Marshmallow Fudge.
RIGHT: One-Bowl Celebration Cake.

Left: Glasses from Waterford Wedgwood.

ONE-BOWL CELEBRATION CAKE

375g butter
2 cups (400g) firmly packed
brown sugar
6 eggs
1.5kg mixed dried fruit
1 cup (210g) glace cherries, halved
¼ cup (60ml) marmalade
¾ cup (180ml) dry sherry
3 cups (450g) plain flour
2 teaspoons mixed spice

BUTTER FROSTING
½ cup (75g) plain flour
1½ cups (375ml) milk
375g soft butter
1½ cups (240g) icing sugar mixture
3 teaspoons vanilla essence

Grease deep 30cm oval cake pan (4 litre/ 16 cup capacity). Line base and side with 3 layers of paper, bringing paper 5cm above edge of pan.

Beat butter and sugar in large bowl with electric mixer until just combined, add eggs 1 at a time, beat only until ingredients are combined between additions. Stir in mixed fruit and cherries, then marmalade, sherry and sifted dry ingredients; mix well.

Spread mixture into prepared pan. Bake in slow oven 3 to 3½ hours. Cover, cool in pan. Spread side and top of cake with butter frosting, refrigerate 30 minutes. Decorate with gold ribbon, or as desired.
Butter Frosting: Blend flour with milk in pan, stir over heat until mixture boils and thickens; cool 2 minutes. Blend or process mixture until smooth, push through fine sieve; cool.

Beat butter, sifted sugar and essence in medium bowl with electric mixer until light and fluffy. Beat in flour mixture. Beat about 6 minutes or until fluffy and spreadable.

Serves 20 to 40.

■ Frosted cake can be made
3 days ahead.
■ Storage: Covered, in refrigerator.
■ Freeze: Unfrosted cake suitable.
■ Microwave: Not suitable

PLUM AND HAZELNUT BREAD PUDDING

10 large (about 1.5kg) plums, halved
⅓ cup (35g) packaged ground
**   hazelnuts, toasted**
18 slices white bread
1 litre (4 cups) milk
1 cup (250ml) cream
1½ cups (330g) castor sugar
1 vanilla bean, split
6 eggs
6 egg yolks
¼ teaspoon ground nutmeg
¼ teaspoon ground cinnamon

Grease 2 shallow ovenproof dishes (2 litre/ 8 cup capacity each). Slice plums thinly. Cover bases of prepared dishes with two-thirds of the plums, sprinkle with half the nuts. Remove crusts from bread, cut slices in half diagonally. Place bread over nuts in overlapping pieces, alternating with remaining plum slices.

Combine milk, cream, sugar and vanilla bean in pan, stir over heat, without boiling, until sugar is dissolved; remove bean.

Whisk eggs, egg yolks and spices together in bowl, gradually whisk in warm milk mixture. Gently pour custard over bread. Place dishes in 2 baking dishes with enough boiling water to come halfway up sides of ovenproof dishes. Bake in moderately slow oven about 50 minutes, or until lightly browned and firm. Remove from baking dishes. Serve sprinkled with remaining nuts.

Serves 12 to 16.

■ Recipe can be made 3 hours ahead.
■ Storage: Room temperature.
■ Freeze: Not suitable.
■ Microwave: Not suitable.

BELOW: From left: Tropical Fruits in Fragrant Lime Syrup, Plum and Hazelnut Bread Pudding.
RIGHT: Coffee Caramel Walnut Cake.

Below: Plates and serviettes from Barbara's Storehouse; forks from Home & Garden on the Mall.
Right: China from Royal Doulton.

TROPICAL FRUITS IN FRAGRANT LIME SYRUP

You need about 6 limes for this recipe.

1 large pineapple, chopped
1 medium red pawpaw, chopped
3 large mangoes, chopped
1kg lychees, peeled
3 medium star fruit, sliced
2 large bananas, sliced
1 cup (150g) macadamias,
  chopped, toasted
500g mascarpone cheese
600ml cream

LIME SYRUP
3 cups (750ml) water
3 cups (660g) castor sugar
2 tablespoons grated lime rind
2 star anise
5 cardamom pods, crushed
1½ tablespoons grated fresh ginger
⅓ cup (80ml) lime juice
1 vanilla bean, split

Combine fruits in large bowl, pour over lime syrup, cover, refrigerate until cold. Serve sprinkled with nuts. Serve with combined cheese and cream.
Lime Syrup: Combine all ingredients in pan, stir over heat, without boiling, until sugar is dissolved. Simmer, without stirring, 15 minutes; cool. Remove star anise, cardamom and vanilla bean.

Serves 10.

■ Lime syrup can be made
  5 days ahead.
■ Storage: Covered, in refrigerator.
■ Freeze: Not suitable.
■ Microwave: Not suitable.

COFFEE CARAMEL WALNUT CAKE

185g butter
1½ cups (330g) castor sugar
4 eggs
1½ cups (225g) plain flour
¼ cup (35g) self-raising flour
1½ tablespoons dry instant coffee
1 tablespoon hot water
¾ cup (180ml) sour cream
600ml thickened cream, whipped

COFFEE WALNUT CARAMEL
400ml can sweetened condensed milk
40g butter
2 tablespoons golden syrup
3 teaspoons dry instant coffee
1 tablespoon hot water
⅔ cup (70g) walnuts, finely chopped

PRALINE
1½ cups (210g) slivered
  almonds, toasted
1½ cups (330g) castor sugar
¾ cup (180ml) water

Grease deep 23cm square cake pan. Beat butter and sugar in large bowl with electric mixer until light and fluffy. Add eggs 1 at a time, beat until combined. Stir in sifted flours, blended coffee and water, and sour cream in 2 batches. Pour mixture into prepared pan, bake in moderately slow oven about 1 hour. Stand 5 minutes before turning onto wire rack to cool.

Cut cake in half to form 2 rectangles. Split each rectangle into 5 even layers. Spread warm coffee walnut caramel over 4 layers of each cake, spread with some of the whipped cream, re-assemble cakes on plates. Refrigerate until firm. Spread with remaining cream, cover with praline; decorate as desired.
Coffee Walnut Caramel: Combine condensed milk, butter, golden syrup and combined coffee and water in pan, stir over heat until butter melts and caramel starts to bubble. Remove from heat, stir in nuts.
Praline: Place nuts on greased oven tray. Combine sugar and water in pan, stir over heat, without boiling, until sugar is dissolved. Bring to boil, boil, uncovered, without stirring, until golden brown, pour over nuts. Stand until set, break into small pieces, process until fine.

Makes 2.

■ Cake can be made a day ahead;
  coat with praline on day of serving.
■ Storage: Covered, in refrigerator.
■ Freeze: Not suitable.
■ Microwave: Not suitable.

MARZIPAN TARTLETS

200g packet pure almond paste
pure icing sugar

FILLING
¾ cup (180ml) thickened cream
200g White Melts, chopped
1 tablespoon Grand Marnier

Lightly oil 12-hole gem scone iron. Roll a third of the paste on surface lightly dusted with sifted icing sugar until 3mm thick. Cut 4cm rounds from paste, place in prepared iron. Bake in moderate oven about 10 minutes or until lightly browned. Stand in iron 5 minutes. Carefully ease around edges of tartlet cases with spatula, place tartlets cases on wire racks to cool. Repeat with remaining paste.

Spoon filling into piping bag fitted with small star tube. Pipe filling into cases, decorate as desired, dust lightly with sifted icing sugar.

Filling: Combine cream, chocolate and liqueur in medium heatproof bowl, stir over pan of simmering water until chocolate is melted. Refrigerate until just thick. Beat with electric mixer until chocolate is just fluffy (do not over-beat).

Makes about 36.

- Cases can be made 2 days ahead. Fill close to serving.
- Storage: Airtight container.
- Freeze: Not suitable.
- Microwave: Filling suitable.

FROZEN MOCHA CHEESECAKE

250g packet plain uniced
**   chocolate biscuits**
125g unsalted butter, melted
1½ cups (210g) slivered
**   almonds, toasted**
300ml thickened cream
¼ cup (40g) icing sugar mixture
250g strawberries
2 teaspoons cocoa
2 teaspoons icing sugar mixture, extra

FILLING
2 teaspoons gelatine
1 tablespoon water
2 tablespoons dry instant coffee
2 tablespoons boiling water
500g packaged cream cheese
2 teaspoons vanilla essence
2 tablespoons Kahlua or Tia Maria
400g can sweetened condensed milk
200g dark chocolate, melted
300ml thickened cream

Grease 23cm springform tin, line base and side with plastic wrap. Process biscuits until finely crushed, stir in butter. Press biscuit mixture over base of prepared tin; refrigerate until firm. Pour filling into crumb crust, freeze until firm.

Process nuts until finely crushed. Remove cheesecake from tin, press nuts firmly around side. Beat cream and icing sugar mixture in small bowl with electric mixer until soft peaks form. Decorate

cheesecake with cream and strawberries; dust with sifted cocoa and extra icing sugar.

Filling: Sprinkle gelatine over the 1 tablespoon of water in cup, stand in pan of simmering water, stir until dissolved. Combine coffee and boiling water in bowl, stir until dissolved. Beat cream cheese in large bowl with electric mixer until smooth. Beat in hot coffee mixture, then essence, liqueur, milk, chocolate and gelatine mixture. Beat cream in small bowl with electric mixer until soft peaks form, fold into chocolate mixture.

Serves 10 to 12.

- Cheesecake with nuts can be made and frozen 2 weeks ahead. Remove from freezer at least 10 minutes before serving.
- Microwave: Gelatine suitable.

PASSIONFRUIT AND GINGER ROULADE

You will need about 24 passionfruit.

5 eggs
¾ cup (165g) castor sugar
1 cup (150g) self-raising flour
3 teaspoons ground ginger
1 tablespoon hot water
50g butter, melted
2 tablespoons castor sugar, extra

PASSIONFRUIT FILLING
⅔ cup (160ml) mascarpone cheese
⅔ cup (160ml) thickened cream
⅓ cup (80ml) passionfruit pulp
2 tablespoons icing sugar mixture
3 teaspoons Grand Marnier

PASSIONFRUIT SAUCE
1¾ cups (430ml) passionfruit pulp
1 cup (220g) castor sugar
¾ cup (180ml) water
1½ teaspoons cornflour
3 teaspoons water, extra

Grease 26cm x 32cm Swiss roll pan, line base and sides with baking paper. Beat eggs in large bowl with electric mixer until thick and creamy. Gradually add sugar, beat until dissolved between additions. Fold in sifted flour and ginger, then combined water and butter. Spread mixture into prepared pan, bake in moderately hot oven about 15 minutes.

Turn sponge onto baking paper sprinkled with extra sugar, trim edges of cake. Roll up cake from long side, stand 2 minutes, unroll; cool. Spread cake with passionfruit filling, roll up, refrigerate 3 hours or until firm. Serve with passionfruit sauce.

Passionfruit Filling: Combine all ingredients in bowl; whisk until slightly thickened.

Passionfruit Sauce: Strain passionfruit pulp, reserve 1½ tablespoons of seeds. You will need 1½ cups (375ml) strained juice for this recipe.

Combine sugar and water in pan, stir over heat, without boiling, until sugar is dissolved, simmer, without stirring, 2 minutes. Add passionfruit juice and reserved seeds, bring to boil, stir in blended cornflour and extra water, stir until mixture boils and thickens; cool.

Serves 10.

- Roulade can be made a day ahead. Passionfruit sauce 3 days ahead.
- Storage: Covered, separately, in refrigerator.
- Freeze: Unfilled roulade suitable.
- Microwave: Not suitable.

ABOVE: Marzipan Tartlets.
RIGHT: From back: Frozen Mocha Cheesecake, Passionfruit and Ginger Roulade.

Above: China from Waterford Wedgwood. Right: Plates from The Bay Tree Kitchen Shop, cake slice from Linen & Lace of Balmain.

BLACK FOREST CAKE

370g packet rich chocolate cake mix
1 cup (250ml) vegetable oil
2½ cups (625ml) water
300g dark chocolate, melted
1 cup (200g) firmly packed
 brown sugar
2 cups (300g) plain flour
½ cup (50g) cocoa
2 eggs
1 teaspoon bicarbonate of soda
900ml thickened cream
½ cup (80g) icing sugar mixture
⅓ cup (80ml) Kirsch
800g can cherries, drained, halved
1½ cups (120g) flaked
 almonds, toasted

Grease deep 28cm round cake pan, line base and side with greased baking paper, bringing paper 5cm above edge of pan. Combine cake mix, oil, water, chocolate, sugar, flour, cocoa, eggs and soda in large bowl, beat on low speed with electric mixer until well combined. Beat on medium speed further 3 minutes. Pour mixture into prepared pan, bake in moderately slow oven about 1½ hours. Stand cake 10 minutes before turning onto wire rack to cool. Cut cake into 3 layers.

Beat cream and icing sugar mixture in medium bowl with electric mixer until soft peaks form. Place a layer of cake on serving plate, brush with a third of the liqueur; spread with ¾ cup (180ml) of cream and half the cherries. Top with another layer of cake, brush with half the remaining liqueur, spread with ¾ cup (180ml) cream and remaining cherries. Top with remaining layer of cake, brush with remaining liqueur. Spread top and side with half the remaining cream, press nuts on side; pipe remaining cream around edge. Decorate with cherries and chocolate curls, if desired. Refrigerate 2 hours before serving.

Serves 20.

- Recipe can be made a day ahead.
- Storage: Covered, in refrigerator.
- Freeze: Undecorated cake suitable.
- Microwave: Not suitable.

CHOC-MINT MERINGUES

3 egg whites
¾ cup (165g) castor sugar
2 x 35g packets peppermint crisp
 bars, chopped

Beat egg whites and sugar in small bowl with electric mixer about 10 minutes or until sugar is dissolved and mixture is stiff and glossy. Fold in peppermint crisps. Drop tablespoons of mixture into small 5cm paper patty cases on oven trays. Bake in very slow oven about 45 minutes or until firm. Cool in oven with door ajar.

Makes about 40.

- Recipe can be made 2 days ahead.
- Storage: Airtight container.
- Freeze: Not suitable.
- Microwave: Not suitable.

ALMOND LACE BISCUITS

60g butter
¼ cup (55g) castor sugar
⅓ cup (80ml) glucose syrup
1 tablespoon honey
⅓ cup (50g) white plain flour
1 tablespoon wholemeal plain flour
½ cup (40g) flaked almonds

Grease 8cm x 26cm bar cake pan, line base and sides with foil; grease foil.

Combine butter, sugar, glucose and honey in small pan, stir over heat, without boiling, until butter is melted and sugar dissolved. Bring to boil, remove from heat, stir in sifted flours, then nuts. Pour mixture into prepared pan, refrigerate 3 hours or until set. Turn mixture out, cut into 1.5cm cubes. Place cubes 10cm apart on greased oven trays, bake in moderately hot oven about 6 minutes or until browned. Cool 1 minute, mould biscuits around rolling pin, cool on rolling pin.

Makes about 48.

- Recipe can be made a week ahead.
- Storage: Airtight container.
- Freeze: Not suitable.
- Microwave: Not suitable.

LEFT: Black Forest Cake.
BELOW: From left: Choc-Mint Meringues, Almond Lace Biscuits.

Below: China from Waterford Wedgwood.
Left: China from Villeroy & Boch.

PARTY MENUS

There are delicious menus here for every occasion, showing some of the limitless ways you can mix and match our recipes, whether for a formal 21st birthday dinner, a wedding at home, a fun cocktail party, a barbecue, or any celebtation you have in mind. Where recipes are marked with ✣, they will need to be increased to suit the number of guests. Now, turn the page for tips on planning a party to remember.

SPECIAL OCCASION PARTY

FOR 50

✣ Smoked Chicken and Olive Tartlets

✣ Mussels with Garlic Pepper Mayonnaise

Spicy Eggplant Fritters with Yogurt Dip

✣ Pepper and Beef Salad

✣ Chicken Nicoise Salad

Salmon Crepe Cakes

✣ Best Pasta Salad

One-Bowl Celebration Cake

✣ Tropical Fruits in Fragrant Lime Syrup

Almond Lace Biscuits

Coffee Meringue Kisses

Rich Mocha Truffles

SUMMER BUFFET

FOR 20

Pepperoni Frittata Slice

Pizza Shortbread Rounds

Seafood Platter

Poppy Seed Blinis with Lamb Salad

Spinach, Pear and Asparagus Salad

Lemony Carrot and Zucchini Sticks

Summer Berry Trifle

Frozen Mocha Cheesecake

EAST MEETS WEST

FOR 10

Pork and Prawn Rolls with
Dipping Sauce

Thai-Style Rare Beef Salad

Mango Ice-Cream Cake with
Caramel Mangoes

ELEGANT DINNER PARTY

FOR 10

Crab Gazpacho

Italian-Style Pork Steaks with Prosciutto

Potato Bake with Red Pepper Sauce

Orange and Leaf Salad with Olive Croutes

Poached Pears with Pastry Twists

COCKTAIL PARTY

FOR 30

Polenta with Creamy Herb Topping

Witlof with Smoked Chicken and Avocado

Mini Lamb Kebabs

Paella-ettes

Mexican Salsa Platter

Cheese and Salami Rolls

Parmesan Fish Strips

Chocolate Marshmallow Fudge

Choc-Mint Meringues

Shortbread Strawberry Hearts

VEGETARIAN FEAST

FOR 10

Baby Onion Tartlets

Spinach and Pasta Terrine

OR

Vegetable Ravioli with Hazelnut Butter

Mushroom Strudels with Garlic Mayonnaise

Eggplant, Kumara and Pepper Salad

Salad Leaves with Horseradish Dressing

Almond Syrup Cake with Cointreau
Ice-Cream

CASUAL HOT 'N' SPICY

FOR 10

Curried Sesame Chicken

Chilli Beef Slice

Green Salad of Your Choice

Passionfruit and Ginger
Roulade

LIGHT LUNCH

FOR 10

Antipasto Platters

Marinated Chicken with
Pecan Butter

Black-Eyed Bean and Rice Salad

Fig and Date Tart

BARBECUE

FOR 10

Seafood Salad with Roasted
Garlic Dressing

Barbecued Lamb with Coriander Pesto

Herbed Polenta Slice

Warm Roasted Tomato and
Onion Salad

Plum and Hazelnut Bread Pudding

WINTER BUFFET

FOR 20

Prosciutto Crepe Cake

Bruschetta with Easy-Mix Toppings

Chicken and Spinach Roulade

Rich Beef Casserole with Baby Vegetables

❖ Salad Leaves with Horseradish
Dressing

Sticky Butternut Flan

Almond Syrup Cake with Cointreau
Ice-Cream

SIT-DOWN FORMAL
CELEBRATION

FOR 20

Gravlax and Carpaccio Canapes

❖ Eggplant and Goats' Cheese Roulade

❖ Chilli Lamb with Sesame Vegetables

❖ Fruity Rice

❖ Chocolate Mousse Cake with
Coffee Anglaise

CASUAL WINTER
SOUP PARTY

FOR 20

Quick 'n' Easy Artichoke Pizzas

Pesto Cheesecake with Caraway Crackers

Butter Bean and Csabai Soup

Pumpkin Soup

❖ Onion and Bacon Rolls

Black Forest Cake

PARTY PLANNING

You can relax and enjoy your own party much more if you plan all the details, make lots of lists and give yourself time to be flexible if you need to change your ideas. Here are our tips for success.

A written plan, starting several days (or months) in advance is the secret of organising your party. First, plan your menu, your budget, your shopping, and the equipment and helpers you need for the event. Lists should include one with items to buy ahead, and another with last minute "perishables". Then plan your cooking timetable, starting with dishes which are suitable to freeze.

MENU PLANNING

Choose your menu to suit:

1. The type of occasion, whether casual, formal, a large party, a buffet, a sit-down dinner, etc.

2. Availability and cost of ingredients.

3. Time allotted for preparation.

4. The number of guests, and whether they have any special likes or dislikes in food.

5. Food is also determined by the guests' appetites; for example, consider the contrast if they were a football team as opposed to a less robust group.

Keep it simple

A good rule is to "keep it simple". There is no point in attempting too much to handle, because the quality will suffer and you will feel stressed.

Few cooks can produce a lot of dishes well at once, so plan things so that about two-thirds of the cooking and preparation can be done in advance. Make a plan of action right down to the last minute and stick to it!

When planning a menu, check:

1. Balance – one of the most common problems is too much rich food. The secret is to limit the size and number of creamy and fatty foods. Aim for plenty of fresh vegetables and fruit, some starch and not too many fatty foods.

2. Check menu content; for example, avoid too many eggs, fish in two courses, fruit in two courses, etc.

3. Colour – look for variety in colour. A common problem is too white a meal; for example, pale soup, fish, rice, ice-cream. Remember that food has to tempt the eyes before it can appeal to the tastebuds.

4. Texture – contrast is all important; for example, serve soft with crunchy.

5. Taste – avoid too many conflicting tastes. Too many different tastes on the one plate lead to a confusion of the palate. Think about the food while you are cooking, and make sure to taste it regularly to correct the seasonings. In most of our recipes we leave the addition of salt and pepper to your taste.

DRINKS

Estimating the amount of drinks you need can be even more difficult than food. You may wish to serve spirits when guests arrive, or simply serve beer and sparkling wine and juice, or alcoholic and non-alcoholic punches.

Wine can be served throughout the meal; we suggest you allow half a 750ml bottle per guest.

As a general rule, serve white wine with white meats and red wine with red meats. Wine, of course, is not obligatory at a meal, for example, with a strong-tasting curry you may prefer to serve cider or beer. Remember to have plenty of mineral water and soft drinks on hand also.

If the budget permits, serve port and liqueurs with coffee.

FOOD PRESENTATION

Follow these easy guidelines:

1. Keep presentation simple – don't over-garnish, it detracts from the appearance of the food rather than adds to it. Also, don't overload serving plates. It is better to refill them during the party.

2. Try to keep the garnishes relevant to the food; for example, garnish with the same type of herbs used in the dish.

3. Keep salads, etc., in the refrigerator until the last minute to maintain their fresh look.

4. Dishes served on platters benefit from centre height – mound food higher in the middle with sides sloping down.

SHOPPING & STORING

Establish a budget for your party, make a shopping list and stick to it. Take a pocket calculator to help keep within your budget.

Put all purchases away as soon as possible, especially fresh and frozen food; this will help prevent wastage.

Shop where there is likely to be a high turnover of goods to ensure they are as fresh as possible. Most vegetables store well in the refrigerator in plastic bags or plastic boxes.

MAKE A TIME PLAN

Arrange for any extra equipment, helpers and drinks several weeks ahead.

Prepare food for the freezer as soon as you can.

Shop for fresh ingredients two to three days ahead, and don't forget the flowers.

When preparing a time plan, consider the kitchen equipment, oven space and cook top available as these will determine the amount of cooking you can do at one time.

Many dishes can be made or prepared several hours ahead and reheated at the last moment. We suggest that you make only one quantity of recipes at a time, that is, if you wish to serve two batches of the same recipe, make each batch separately as most households do not have pots and pans large enough for big quantities.

EQUIPMENT & HELPERS

If you are having a large party, consider the "accessories" you need. Have you enough serving plates and china, cutlery, tables, chairs, glasses, linen and so on?

Perhaps friends and relatives can help you with china, cutlery and glasses, but it may be more convenient to hire the things you need. It's best to shop around before hiring; we found wide variations in prices.

Order well in advance and agree on a delivery date; ideally, the day before the party. Around Christmas and other busy times of the year it is best to make orders well in advance.

When hiring glasses, order extra; people put glasses down and walk away from them.

For a formal party or a large function, think of hiring someone to serve and clean up, if your budget will run to it. This will relieve some of the pressure and allow you to enjoy your own party more. Even someone to look after the drinks will help. Again, it is best to shop around first.

GLOSSARY

Here are some terms, names and alternatives to help everyone use and understand our recipes perfectly.

ALCOHOL: is optional, but gives a particular flavour. Use fruit juice or water instead.

ALLSPICE: pimento in ground form.

ALMOND PASTE: almond-flavoured cake paste or prepared marzipan.

ALMONDS:

Flaked: sliced nuts.

Ground: we used packaged, commercially ground nuts unless otherwise specified.

Slivered: nuts cut lengthways.

BACON RASHERS: bacon slices.

BAKING POWDER: is a raising agent consisting of an alkali and an acid. It is mostly made from cream of tartar and bicarbonate of soda in the proportions of 1 level teaspoon of cream of tartar to ½ level teaspoon bicarbonate of soda. This is equivalent to 2 level teaspoons baking powder.

BEETROOT: regular round beet.

BICARBONATE OF SODA: baking soda.

BLACK-EYED BEANS: black-eyed peas.

BOK CHOY: Chinese chard.

BURGHUL: also known as cracked wheat.

BUTTER: use salted or unsalted (also called sweet) butter; 125g is equal to 1 stick butter.

BUTTERFLY: ask your butcher to remove bone and "butterfly" the meat so that it lies flat.

BUTTERMILK: made by adding a culture to skim milk; skim milk can be substituted.

CASSIS: blackcurrant-flavoured liqueur.

CELERIAC: tuberous root with brown skin, white flesh and a celery-like flavour.

CELLOPHANE NOODLES: shiny, thin, translucent noodles made from mung beans.

CHICK PEAS: garbanzos.

CHILLIES: fresh chillies are available in many different types and sizes. Use rubber gloves when chopping fresh chillies.

Flakes, dried: available at Asian food stores.

Powder: the Asian variety is the hottest and is made from ground chillies. It can be used as a substitute for fresh chillies in the proportions of ½ teaspoon ground chilli powder to 1 medium chopped fresh chilli.

CHOCOLATE:

Choc Melts: are discs of dark, compounded chocolate ideal for melting and moulding.

Dark: good-quality cooking chocolate.

Milk: we used good-quality milk chocolate.

White: we used Milky Bar.

CHORIZO SAUSAGE: spicy pork sausage.

COCOA: cocoa powder.

COCONUT: desiccated coconut.

Cream: available in cans and cartons.

Flaked: flaked coconut flesh.

Milk: available in cans from supermarkets.

COINTREAU: orange-flavoured liqueur.

CORIANDER: also known as cilantro and Chinese parsley.

CORN CHIPS: packaged snack food.

CORNFLOUR: cornstarch.

CORNMEAL: ground corn (maize); similar to polenta but pale yellow and finer. One can be substituted for the other, but results will be slightly different.

CORN SYRUP, DARK: an imported product available from supermarkets, delicatessens and health food stores.

COUSCOUS: cereal made from semolina.

CREAM: light pouring cream, also known as half and half.

Sour: a thick commercially cultured soured cream.

Thickened (whipping): double cream or cream with more than 35 percent fat can be used.

CSABAI: mild, Hungarian-style salami seasoned with peppercorns and paprika.

EGGPLANT: aubergine.

ESSENCE: extract.

FILLO PASTRY: tissue-thin pastry bought chilled or frozen.

FISH SAUCE: made from the liquid drained from salted, fermented anchovies. Has a strong smell and taste; use sparingly.

FIVE SPICE POWDER: a pungent mixture of ground spices which include cinnamon, cloves, fennel, star anise and hot peppers.

FLOUR:

Rice: flour made from rice; ground rice can be substituted.

Rye: flour milled from rye.

White plain: unbleached all-purpose flour.

White self-raising: substitute plain (all-purpose) flour and baking powder in the proportions of 1 cup (150g) plain flour to 2 level teaspoons baking powder. Sift together several times before using.

Wholemeal plain: wholewheat all-purpose flour without the addition of baking powder.

FLOUR TORTILLAS: thin, round, unleavened bread available from supermarkets.

GARAM MASALA: varied combinations of cardamom, cinnamon, cloves, coriander, cumin and nutmeg make up this spice.

GHEE: a pure butter fat available in cans; it can be heated to high temperatures.

GHERKIN: cornichon.

GINGER:

Fresh, green or root ginger: scrape off skin and grate, chop or slice as required.

Ground: is available but should not be substituted for fresh ginger in any recipe.

Pickled: vinegared ginger in paper-thin shavings.

GLUCOSE SYRUP (liquid glucose): made from a mixture of sugars.

GOLDEN SYRUP: maple, pancake syrup or honey can be substituted.

GRAND MARNIER: orange-flavoured liqueur.

GRAVLAX: marinated, uncooked salmon.

GREEN GINGER WINE: an Australian-made alcoholic sweet wine infused with finely ground ginger.

GREEN PEPPERCORNS: available in cans or jars, pickled in brine.

HERBS: we have specified when to use fresh or dried herbs. We used dried (not ground) herbs in the proportions of 1:4 for fresh herbs; e.g., 1 teaspoon dried herbs instead of 4 teaspoons (1 tablespoon) chopped fresh herbs.

HOI SIN SAUCE: thick, sweet Chinese barbecue sauce made from salted black beans, onion and garlic.

HORSERADISH, PREPARED: grated horseradish with flavourings.

KAHLUA: coffee-flavoured liqueur.

KIRSCH: cherry-flavoured liqueur.

KUMARA: orange sweet potato.

LAMB PROSCIUTTO: uncooked, unsmoked, cured lamb; ready to eat when bought.

LEMON GRASS: available from Asian food stores and needs to be bruised or chopped before using. Also available in jars.

LEMON PEPPER: a blend of crushed black pepper, lemon, herbs and spices.

LENTILS: dried pulses. There are many varieties, usually identified and named after their colour.

MACADAMIAS: Queensland nuts or Hawaiian nuts.

MARSALA: sweet, fortified wine.

MARZIPAN: smooth, firm, almond-flavoured confectionery paste.

MASCARPONE: a fresh, unripened, smooth, triple cream cheese with a rich sweet taste, slightly acidic.

MIRIN: sweet rice wine used in Japanese cooking. Substitute 1 teaspoon sugar and 1 teaspoon dry sherry for each tablespoon of mirin.

MIXED FRUIT: a combination of sultanas, raisins, currants, mixed peel and cherries.

MIXED SPICE: a blend of ground cinnamon, allspice and nutmeg.

MOLASSES: dark, viscous liquid; the end product of raw sugar manufacturing or refining.

MUSHROOMS:
Button: small, unopened mushrooms with a delicate flavour.
Flat: large, soft, flat mushrooms with a rich, earthy flavour.
Oyster: pale, grey-white mushrooms.
Shitake: used mainly in Chinese and Japanese cooking.
Swiss brown: brown cultivated mushrooms.

Mushrooms, clockwise from left: Oyster, flat, Swiss brown, shitake, button.

MUSSELS: must be tightly closed when bought, indicating they are alive. Before cooking, scrub the shells with a strong brush and remove the "beards". Discard any shells that do not open after cooking.
MUSTARD:
Dijon: a hot French mustard.
Dry: available in powder form.
French: plain mild mustard.
Seeded: a French-style mustard with crushed mustard seeds.
Seeds: can be black or white.
OLIVE OIL:
Extra light/light: mild tasting, light in flavour, colour and aroma, but not lower in kilojoules.
Extra virgin/virgin: the highest quality oils obtained from the first pressing of the olives.
Olive: a blend of refined and virgin olive oils, especially good for everyday cooking.
OLIVE PASTE: is made from olives, olive oil, salt, vinegar and herbs.
OYSTER SAUCE: a rich, brown sauce made from oysters cooked in salt and soy sauce.
PALM SUGAR: very fine sugar from the coconut palm. It is sold in cakes, also known as gula jawa, gula melaka and jaggery. You can use brown or black sugar instead.
PANCETTA: cured pork belly; bacon can be substituted.
PARSLEY, FLAT-LEAFED: also known as continental parsley or Italian parsley.
PEARL BARLEY: barley which has had most of its outer husk removed.
PEPPERMINT CRISP BARS: peppermint cracknel covered in milk chocolate; available from supermarkets.
PEPPERONI: sausage made of minced pork and beef with added fat and hot red pepper.
PEPPERS: capsicum or bell peppers.
PIMIENTOS: canned or bottled peppers.
PINE NUTS: small, cream-coloured, soft kernels with a sweet flavour.
PITTA POCKET BREAD: 2-layered flat bread.
POLENTA: see Cornmeal.
PRAWNS: shrimp.

PROSCIUTTO: uncooked, unsmoked ham cured in salt; ready to eat when bought.
PRUNES: whole dried plums.
PUMPKIN: we used several varieties; any type can be substituted for the other.
QUAIL: game birds from about 250g to 300g.
READY-ROLLED PUFF PASTRY: frozen sheets of puff pastry available from supermarkets.
READY-ROLLED SHORTCRUST PASTRY: frozen sheets of shortcrust pastry available from supermarkets.
RED KIDNEY BEANS: have a floury texture and fairly sweet flavour; colour can vary from pink to maroon.
RED SPANISH ONION: large, purplish-red onion.
REFRIED BEANS: available in cans.
RICE:
Basmati: similar appearance to long-grain rice with a fine aroma.
White: is hulled and polished, can be short- or long-grained.
Wild: from North America, but not a member of the rice family.
RIND: zest.
ROLLED OATS: flattened flakes of grain.
SAFFRON: available in strands or ground form. The quality varies greatly.
SALT:
Celery: mixture of salt and ground celery seeds.
Cooking: coarse, free-running refined salt.
Sea: mixture of salts produced by the evaporation of sea water.
SAMBAL OELEK: paste of chillies and salt.
SEASONED PEPPER: a combination of black pepper, sugar and bell pepper.
SESAME OIL: made from roasted, crushed white sesame seeds. Do not use for frying.
SESAME SEEDS: there are 2 types, black and white; we use both varieties in this book.
SHALLOTS:
Golden: very small member of the onion family with strong flavour.
Green: also known as scallions and spring onions.
SHRIMP PASTE: a powerful, dark brown flavouring made from salted dried shrimp.
SILVERBEET: (Swiss chard) dark green, glossy leaves and white stems.
SNOW PEAS: also known as mange tout (eat all), sugar peas or Chinese peas.
SPECK: smoked pork.
SPINACH, English: a soft-leaved vegetable, more delicate in taste than silverbeet; young silverbeet can be substituted.
SPONGE FINGER BISCUITS: also known as savoiardi.
STAR ANISE: dried, star-shaped fruit of an evergreen tree; it has an aniseed flavour.
STOCK POWDER: 1 cup stock is the equivalent of 1 cup (250ml) water plus 1 crumbled stock cube (or 1 teaspoon stock powder). If you prefer to make your own fresh stock, see recipes on following page.
SUGAR:
We used coarse, granulated table sugar, also known as crystal (white) sugar.

Brown: a soft, fine, granulated sugar containing molasses.
Castor: also known as superfine; is fine, granulated table sugar.
Icing: also known as confectioners' sugar or powdered sugar. We used icing sugar mixture, not pure icing sugar, unless specified.
SUGAR SNAP PEAS: small pods with small, formed peas inside.
SULTANAS: seedless white raisins.
SWEETENED CONDENSED MILK: we used canned milk from which 60% of the water had been removed; the remaining milk is then sweetened with sugar.
SWEET SAKE: Japan's favourite rice wine.
TABASCO SAUCE: made with vinegar, hot red peppers and salt. Use in drops.
TAHINI PASTE: made from sesame seeds.
TAMARIND SAUCE: if unavailable, soak about 30g dried tamarind in a cup of hot water, stand 10 minutes, allow to cool, squeeze pulp dry and use the flavoured water.
TANDOORI PASTE: Indian blend of hot and fragrant spices.
TERIYAKI SAUCE: based on light Japanese soy sauce; contains sugar, spices and vinegar.
TIA MARIA: coffee-flavoured liqueur.
TOMATO:
Paste: a concentrated tomato puree used in flavouring soups, stews and sauces, etc.
Puree: is canned, pureed tomatoes (not tomato paste). Use fresh, peeled, pureed tomatoes as a substitute, if preferred.
Sun-dried: dried tomatoes, sometimes bottled in oil.
UNPROCESSED BRAN: coarse outer layer of grains removed during milling.
V8 VEGETABLE JUICE: tomato-based vegetable juice available in cans.
VINEGAR: we used both white and brown (malt) vinegar in this book.
Balsamic: originated in Modena, Italy. Regional wine is specially processed then aged in antique wooden casks.
Cider: made from apples.
Red wine: vinegar made from the fermentation of red grapes.
Rice: a colourless, seasoned vinegar containing sugar and salt.
Tarragon: fresh tarragon is infused in white wine vinegar.
WASABI PASTE: a very hot Japanese condiment made from a root similar to the horseradish root with bright green flesh.
WATER CHESTNUTS: small, white, crisp bulbs with a brown skin. Canned water chestnuts are peeled and will keep for about a month in the refrigerator.
WITLOF: chicory or Belgian endive.
WORCESTERSHIRE SAUCE: spicy sauce used mainly on red meat.
YEAST: allow 2 teaspoons (7g) dried yeast to each 15g compressed yeast if substituting one for the other.
ZUCCHINI: courgette.

MAKE YOUR OWN STOCK

BEEF STOCK

2kg meaty beef bones
2 onions
2 sticks celery, chopped
2 carrots, chopped
3 bay leaves
2 teaspoons black peppercorns
5 litres (20 cups) water
3 litres (12 cups) water, extra

Place bones and unpeeled chopped onions in baking dish. Bake, uncovered, in hot oven about 1 hour or until bones and onions are well browned. Transfer bones and onions to large pan, add celery, carrots, bay leaves, peppercorns and water, simmer, uncovered, 3 hours. Add extra water, simmer, uncovered, further 1 hour; strain.
Makes about 2.5 litres (10 cups).

■ Stock can be made 4 days ahead.
■ Storage: Covered, in refrigerator.
■ Freeze: Suitable.
■ Microwave: Not suitable.

CHICKEN STOCK

2kg chicken bones
2 onions, chopped
2 sticks celery, chopped
2 carrots, chopped
3 bay leaves
2 teaspoons black peppercorns
5 litres (20 cups) water

Combine all ingredients in large pan, simmer, uncovered, 2 hours; strain.
Makes about 2.5 litres (10 cups).

■ Stock can be made 4 days ahead.
■ Storage: Covered, in refrigerator.
■ Freeze: Suitable.
■ Microwave: Not suitable.

FISH STOCK

1½kg fish bones
3 litres (12 cups) water
1 onion, chopped
2 sticks celery, chopped
2 bay leaves
1 teaspoon black peppercorns

Combine all ingredients in large pan, simmer, uncovered, 20 minutes; strain.
Makes about 2.5 litres (10 cups).

■ Stock can be made 4 days ahead.
■ Storage: Covered, in refrigerator.
■ Freeze: Suitable.
■ Microwave: Not suitable.

VEGETABLE STOCK

1 large carrot, chopped
1 large parsnip, chopped
2 onions, chopped
6 sticks celery, chopped
4 bay leaves
2 teaspoons black peppercorns
3 litres (12 cups) water

Combine all ingredients in large pan, simmer, uncovered, 1½ hours; strain.
Makes about 1.25 litres (5 cups).

■ Stock can be made 4 days ahead.
■ Storage: Covered, in refrigerator.
■ Freeze: Suitable.
■ Microwave: Not suitable.

INDEX

QUICK CONVERSION GUIDE

Wherever you live in the world you can use our recipes with the help of our easy-to-follow conversions for all your cooking needs. These conversions are approximate only. The difference between the exact and approximate conversions of liquid and dry measures amounts to only a teaspoon or two, and will not make any difference to your cooking results.

MEASURING EQUIPMENT

The difference between measuring cups internationally is minimal within 2 or 3 teaspoons' difference. (For the record, 1 Australian metric measuring cup will hold approximately 250ml.) The most accurate way of measuring dry ingredients is to weigh them. When measuring liquids use a clear glass or plastic jug with metric markings.

If you would like the measuring cups and spoons as used in our Test Kitchen, turn to page 128 for details and order coupon. In this book we use metric measuring cups and spoons approved by Standards Australia.

● a graduated set of four cups for measuring dry ingredients; the sizes are marked on the cups.
● a graduated set of four spoons for measuring dry and liquid ingredients; the amounts are marked on the spoons.
● 1 TEASPOON: 5ml.
● 1 TABLESPOON: 20ml.

NOTE: NZ, CANADA, USA AND UK ALL USE 15ml TABLESPOONS.
ALL CUP AND SPOON MEASUREMENTS ARE LEVEL.

DRY MEASURES

METRIC	IMPERIAL
15g	½oz
30g	1oz
60g	2oz
90g	3oz
125g	4oz (¼lb)
155g	5oz
185g	6oz
220g	7oz
250g	8oz (½lb)
280g	9oz
315g	10oz
345g	11oz
375g	12oz (¾lb)
410g	13oz
440g	14oz
470g	15oz
500g	16oz (1lb)
750g	24oz (1½lb)
1kg	32oz (2lb)

LIQUID MEASURES

METRIC	IMPERIAL
30ml	1 fluid oz
60ml	2 fluid oz
100ml	3 fluid oz
125ml	4 fluid oz
150ml	5 fluid oz (¼ pint/1 gill)
190ml	6 fluid oz
250ml	8 fluid oz
300ml	10 fluid oz (½ pint)
500ml	16 fluid oz
600ml	20 fluid oz (1 pint)
1000ml (1 litre)	1¾ pints

WE USE LARGE EGGS WITH AN AVERAGE WEIGHT OF 60g

HELPFUL MEASURES

METRIC	IMPERIAL
3mm	⅛in
6mm	¼in
1cm	½in
2cm	¾in
2.5cm	1in
5cm	2in
6cm	2½in
8cm	3in
10cm	4in
13cm	5in
15cm	6in
18cm	7in
20cm	8in
23cm	9in
25cm	10in
28cm	11in
30cm	12in (1ft)

HOW TO MEASURE

When using the graduated metric measuring cups, it is important to shake the dry ingredients loosely into the required cup. Do not tap the cup on the bench, or pack the ingredients into the cup unless otherwise directed. Level top of cup with knife. When using graduated metric measuring spoons, level top of spoon with knife. When measuring liquids in the jug, place jug on flat surface, check for accuracy at eye level.

OVEN TEMPERATURES

These oven temperatures are only a guide; we've given you the lower degree of heat. Always check the manufacturer's manual.

	C° (Celsius)	F° (Fahrenheit)	Gas Mark
Very slow	120	250	1
Slow	150	300	2
Moderately slow	160	325	3
Moderate	180	350	4
Moderately hot	190	375	5
Hot	200	400	6
Very hot	230	450	7